Ready-to-Use Activities for Teaching JULIUS CAESAR

Ready-to-Use Activities for Teaching JULIUS CAESAR

JOHN WILSON SWOPE

**THE CENTER FOR APPLIED
RESEARCH IN EDUCATION**
West Nyack, New York 10995

© 1993 *by*

THE CENTER FOR APPLIED
RESEARCH IN EDUCATION
West Nyack, New York

10 9 8 7 6 5 4 3 2 1

Library of Congress Cataloging-in-Publication Data

Swope, John Wilson.
　　Ready-to-use activities for teaching Julius Caesar / by John
Wilson Swope.
　　　　　p.　　cm. — (Shakespeare teacher's activities library)
　　Includes bibliographical references.
　　ISBN 0-87628-117-X
　　　　1. Shakespeare, William, 1564-1616.　　Julius Caesar.
　　2. Shakespeare, William, 1564-1616—Study and teaching (Secondary)
　　3. Caesar, Julius, in fiction, drama, poetry, etc.—Study and teaching.
　　4. Rome in literature—Study and teaching.　　5. Activity programs in education.
　　I. Title.　　II. Series: Swope, John Wilson.
　　Shakespeare teacher's activities library.
　　PR2808.S96　　1993
　　822.3'3—dc20　　　　　　　　　　　　　　　　　　　　　　　93-5221
　　　　　　　　　　　　　　　　　　　　　　　　　　　　　　　　　CIP

ISBN 0-87628-117-X

**The Center for Applied Research
in Education,** Professional Publishing
West Nyack, New York 10995
Simon & Schuster, A Paramount Communications Company

Printed in the United States of America

Dedication

To my mentors, friends, and colleagues:
Patricia Proudfoot Kelly and Robert C. Small, Jr.

About the Author

In addition to eleven years as a middle and secondary English, speech, and drama teacher, John Wilson Swope has taught English education courses at the University of Florida and the University of Northern Iowa, where he is currently an assistant professor of English. His articles and reviews have appeared in *English Journal, English Leadership Quarterly, FOCUS, The Leaflet,* and *The Virginia English Bulletin.* He is a frequent presenter at conferences sponsored by the National Council of Teachers in English and its local affiliates. As an actor, director, and designer, he has participated in more than a dozen community theater productions.

About This Resource

Shakespeare's *Julius Caesar,* like *Romeo and Juliet, Hamlet,* and *Macbeth,* is a common choice among literature programs. As teachers, we enjoy these works and think them important for more than their stories. For me, Shakespeare's ability to observe human nature and convey it through language commands my attention. His characters act and interact with others in ways that I recognize around me. His poetry conveys human experience through timeless literacy form.

Although we prize Shakespeare's plays, they present many problems for our students as first-time readers. As teachers, we want our students to comprehend the plot, understand the motives of the characters, appreciate the language, and decipher countless allusions—sometimes after only a single reading.

Before many students study *Julius Caesar,* they have already studied another play, most often *Romeo and Juliet.* These students aren't expert with Elizabethan language or conventions of blank verse; however, they possess knowledge and personal experience to help them understand and appreciate the play. A generation ago when students also studied Caesar's *Commentaries on the Gallic Wars* in Latin classes, Julius Caesar was a much more familiar historical personage than he is today. However, teenage readers can identify with many of the situations, characters, and themes within Shakespeare's *Julius Caesar.* They may have either betrayed a friendship or been betrayed by a friend, so they can identify with Brutus' struggle to assassinate Caesar in order to continue the Roman Republic. Within their own school and community, they can identify persons who seem as pompous as Caesar, as honest as Brutus, as simple as Casca, and as cunning as Cassius. As teenagers, they know firsthand about struggles for power and autonomy. When we help students recall, organize, and share their relevant knowledge and experience, it becomes a valuable resource for them to begin understanding, appreciating, and interpreting the play.

As with other volumes in *the Shakespeare Teacher's Activities Library, Ready-to-Use Activities for Julius Caesar* is a collection of student-centered activities for presenting the play to first-time readers. I've designed these activities to help students recall prior knowledge and personal experience that they can relate to the play. When students have little prior knowledge or experience that they can relate to the play, I have designed activities—like the plot summaries, scenarios for improvisation, or prereading vocabulary—to create or enhance their knowledge.

Although students expect structure in a classroom, they tend to dislike routine. This resource presents choices of activities to help students make connections between their lives and Shakespeare's *Julius Caesar.* The activities afford students opportunities to read, write, think, speak, and act out in response to the play.

In developing these activities, I've drawn upon research in effective teaching, reading, whole language, and English education as well as my experience as a classroom teacher. I have also had the opportunities to team teach with my friends and colleagues, Sue Ellen Savereide, instructor at the Malcolm Price Laboratory

School, Cedar Falls, Iowa, and Sharon Palas, English teacher at Denver High School, Denver, Iowa, in developing these materials.

Although these activities will help get your students involved with Julius Caesar, I don't propose that these are the only ones that work with students. As the teacher, you determine which activities the students use, and whether they work individually, in pairs, small groups, or as a whole class. You also need to decide whether the students read silently, aloud, or in combination. I also encourage you to continue using the films and professional recordings of the play that have worked in the past, for both films and recordings may be used as prereading, reading, or postreading techniques. In addition to the ideas I present here, I urge you to develop your own specific improvisations, questions, and extending activities that reflect your specific teaching objectives and that best fit your district's curriculum.

John Wilson Swope

Table of Contents

ACT II

PART THREE: APPENDICES

PART ONE

━━━━━━━━━━━━━━ ❧ ━━━━━━━━━━━━━━

Suggestions to the Teacher

Reading Processes

Rationale

Organization of Activities

Prereading Activities

During-Reading Activities

Postreading Activities

Extending Activities

Summary of Reading Process
    Activities for *Julius Caesar*

A Guide to Using This Resource

READING PROCESSES

In recent years, teachers have come to teach writing as a process of prewriting, writing, and rewriting. Approaching reading as a similar process of prereading, during reading, and postreading allows students to approach difficult texts systematically, enhancing their comprehension, understanding, and appreciation. As a linguistic process, effective reading involves the reader: the reader anticipates what the text may reveal, reads to confirm or contradict those goals, and then thinks about what has been read.

To guide you in using reading as a process to teach *Julius Caesar,* this section will

- explain reading processes,
- establish a rationale for using reading as a process in studying the play,
- explain the overall organization of the student activities, and
- explain the function of each of the activities in this resource.

All activities follow a reading processes model and fall into the following three major groups, with a fourth group of optional activities called *extending activities.*

Prereading activities help students assess and organize information or personal experience that relates to what they will read. These activities help students to connect their prior knowledge to the text as well as help them to establish a genuine purpose for reading it.

During-reading activities encourage students to read actively rather than passively, taking more responsibility for their own learning. Because full comprehension of a text doesn't occur immediately upon reading it the first time, students often need help to make sense of what they've just read. By structuring reading sessions and using reading, writing, speaking, listening, viewing, and critical thinking activities to foster active contemplation of the text, students can begin to explore their possible interpretations of the text.

Postreading activities help students make sense of their earlier explorations of the literature and come to an overall understanding of a work.

Extending activities allow students to apply what they've learned about the text to new situations after they've reached an understanding of the work.

RATIONALE

Reading *Julius Caesar* is difficult, even for the most proficient students. As teachers, when we read the play along with our students, we may be reading the text for the tenth or twentieth time. We may forget that our students are encountering this text for the first time. As teachers and students of literature ourselves, we have developed our appreciation, understanding, interpretations, and love of Shakespeare's plays through our repeated exposure to them. We have read, reread, contemplated, researched, discussed, listened to, and viewed performances of them. The activities in this resource apply a reading process approach to the study of *Julius Caesar* and encourage students to read, reread, contemplate, discuss, listen to, and view the play as active readers and learners, enhancing their understanding, appreciation, and enjoyment of it.

This resource provides you with choices of activities to help students understand *Julius Caesar*. The selection of activities depends upon the students you teach, your instructional goals, and the time you wish to devote to the study of the play. For example, a unit using these materials would include

- 🙶 completing one focusing activity and reviewing the plot summary for a specific scene as a prereading activity,

- 🙶 keeping either a character diary or a response journal throughout the reading of the play as a during-reading activity,

- 🙶 completing one of the postreading activities.

The vocabulary, viewing a scene on videotape, guides to character development, critical thinking questions, language exploration, and extending activities are other options to achieve additional instructional goals.

ORGANIZATION OF ACTIVITIES

To facilitate the planning of your unit, I've grouped the students' activities according to act. For each act, I've arranged the activities according to the stage of the reading process—prereading, during-reading, postreading. (See Figure 1: Summary of Reading Process Activities for *Julius Caesar* located at the end of Part One.) Extending activities, designed for use only after a complete reading of the play, follow the materials for Act V. Answer keys for quizzes and suggested answers for discussion activities are located in the appendices.

PREREADING ACTIVITIES

The prereading activities for *Julius Caesar* include focusing activities, plot summaries, and vocabulary.

Focusing Activities

All focusing activities share a common goal: to help students organize and apply relevant prior knowledge and experience to the scene they are about to read. Because they set the stage for reading, they should be brief, generally between five and ten minutes. These activities help establish a genuine purpose for reading by encouraging students to speculate about what *may* happen rather than to predict accurately what *does happen* in the play. Although several different focusing activities are available for each scene of the play, students need to complete *only one* of them:

scenarios for improvisation, prereading discussion questions, speculation journal, or introducing the play with videotape.

Scenarios for Improvisation. These improvisational group activities take a few minutes for students to prepare and present but allow them to explore possible motives and actions of characters in situations that relate to a particular scene. Once they present an improvisation to the class, it becomes a common experience and a part of each person's relevant prior knowledge. A brief discussion of the improvisation will help connect the improvisation to the action of the play. After reading, the students may wish to discuss the similarities between the improvisation and what actually happened in the scene.

Prereading Discussion Questions. As an anticipatory device, these questions allow students to talk through their speculations about what they will read. The questions tend to be more effective once everyone has become familiar with a play and its characters.

Speculation Journal. This activity begins as an individual writing-to-learn activity. After students speculate for three to five minutes about what *might* happen, encourage them to share their predictions. Keep in mind that the goal is for them to use what they know about characters and motivations, to explore what logically *could* happen and not to guess correctly what *does* happen.

Introducing the Play with Videotape. Showing the opening scenes of a play before students begin reading it can be an excellent introductory focusing activity. A visual presentation provides them with a sense of the setting and overall action of the scene before they confront the written text. After showing the film or tape, ask the class, "What seems to be going on here?" A few minutes' discussion will help you determine if the class has a general sense of what they've seen.

Plot Summaries

Once students have completed a focusing activity, share the plot summary of the scene with them before they begin reading it. Reading the summary helps students establish the overall direction for the scene before beginning Shakespeare's verse. With the summary as a road map, students are less likely to get lost among Shakespeare's many literary allusions.

Vocabulary

The vocabulary activities allow students to expand their vocabularies through repeated exposure to words within context. The words defined in the prereading lists are the bases for both of the postreading vocabulary activities: vocabulary in context and vocabulary review quiz. Although most of the words on these lists are in common use today, Shakespeare often used them in different contexts than contemporary speakers do. The lists provide brief definitions and synonyms as well as a sentence to illustrate the word in a context similar to the one the students will encounter in the play.

DURING-READING ACTIVITIES

Students need to read actively. When the text is as challenging as *Julius Caesar,* few students can comprehend it immediately. Instead, most of them need to contemplate the text consciously to make sense of it. During-reading activities allow them to reread, write, talk, listen, view, and think about what they've just read.

Four types of activities enable students to contemplate actively what they've just read and begin to explore possible interpretations of it: *response journal, character diary, viewing scenes on videotape,* and *guides to character development.*

Response Journal

This writing-to-learn activity is based upon the work of David Bleich. The students make four types of responses either while they read or immediately upon completing the reading of a particular scene. They respond emotionally to what they're reading and try to speculate why the text provokes a particular response. Then they record and explore their own associations and experiences that relate to the text. The figurative response then draws the students back to the text, making them contemplate an important section of it. Finally, the response journal encourages students to record the questions that arise while they read, so they can address them later.

All students keep an individual response journal throughout their reading of *Julius Caesar.* They can use it as a means to record their reactions to what they read either while they read or immediately upon completing a reading session. For example, if students read the play aloud during class, encourage them to take the last few minutes of the period to write in their response journals. If students are to read outside of class, then also have them complete their response journals as part of the homework assignment. The writing in the response journal is exploratory in nature: it is a forum for formulating and testing hypotheses about the play, its language, and its characters; it is not a place where grammar, usage, and mechanics are an issue.

Character Diary

An alternative to the response journal, this exploratory writing-to-learn activity encourages students to read actively and to contemplate what they've read. The students summarize the action of the play, in the form of a personal diary, from the perspective of a minor character. Because no character is present for all the action of a play, the character diary requires students to provide a logical account of how their individual character comes to know the action. This paraphrasing not only improves students' reading comprehension but affects a broad range of related language skills, "including literal recall of events, characters, main points, rhetorical features, stylistic devices and text structure" (Brown and Cambourne, 9). Like the response journal, the writing in the character diary is exploratory in nature.

Viewing a Scene on Videotape

As an optional during-reading activity, students view and discuss several scenes immediately after having read them. These include Brutus and Cassius' first discussing Caesar's increasing power (Act I, scene ii), Brutus' deciding to join the conspiracy (Act II, scene i), Caesar's assassination and funeral (Act III, scenes i and ii), and Brutus and Cassius' quarrel (Act IV, scenes ii and iii).

Because the students will already be familiar with the play's language, action, and characters, viewing the scene permits them to use the additional visual and auditory information to improve their understanding of the play's language and characters. For example, seeing professional actors portray Brutus and Cassius's first meeting demonstrates the skill with which Cassius can suggest treason without committing it. Similarly, letting students see professional actors deliver Brutus' and Antony's funeral orations bring the language to life.

Guides to Character Development

These guides are additional means to structure the students' contemplation of a play. Five sets of guides to character development and revelation include Antony, Brutus, and Cassius as major characters and Caesar and Portia as minor ones.

How you use these activities depends on the specific goals for studying *Julius Caesar*. You may have the entire class examine how Shakespeare develops a major character by having them choose to examine Antony, Brutus, or Cassius. Similarly, they may examine how Shakespeare reveals minor, and more static, characters like Caesar or Portia. Have them complete these activities individually, in pairs, or in small groups.

These charts direct students first to review specific portions of the play to determine what characters do, say, or what other characters say about them before drawing conclusions about what insight this information provides into a specific character. You will find charts for the characters with the during-reading materials for each act in which the specific character appears. Antony, Brutus, and Cassius in all five acts, Caesar in the first three, but Portia only in Acts II and IV.

POSTREADING ACTIVITIES

Postreading activities help students read, write, talk, or act their ways through the play to reach an overall understanding of it. This resource provides four types of postreading activities: *comprehension checks, critical thinking questions, language exploration,* and *vocabulary.*

Comprehension Checks

Two types of activities assess students' comprehension of the text that they've read: a multiple choice quiz and small group discussion questions.

Comprehension Check (multiple choice). The quizzes consist of five multiple choice questions for each act. Two are factual, two are interpretative, and one is evaluative.

Small Group Discussion Questions to Check Comprehension. These questions help students assess whether they understand key issues of a play. Encourage them to discuss their answers with one another and return to the text to clarify misunderstandings through collaborative discussion in small groups.

Critical Thinking Questions

Postreading discussion questions are probably the most common activity in a literature classroom. However, questions need to do more than simply check whether the students have read a particular passage. The Critical Thinking Questions follow the model of Christenbury and Kelly and help students connect the act that they've just read with the play as a whole, to their personal experiences, and to other literary experiences. To establish the goal for the discussion, present the focus question first. Although this question is the one that students will find difficult to answer at first, present it to them and just let them think about it. Explore the related issues in the other questions and then have the students return to the focus question to connect their other responses to it.

Language Exploration

These activities allow students to return to the text and explore how Shakespeare uses language within the context of the acts of the play that they've already read. You can encourage them to use these activities to review and apply concepts and to develop interpretations of specific passages. The concepts in *Julius Caesar* include a review of figurative language (simile, metaphor, personification, and apostrophe), symbol, verbal irony, and irony of situation.

Vocabulary Activities

Vocabulary in Context. For a postreading activity, students can examine how Shakespeare uses the prereading vocabulary within a specific passage. Then, the students can apply an appropriate meaning and develop an interpretation of the passage within the context of the play. Although these activities direct students to excerpts, you might encourage students to review an entire section of the particular scene to establish a more complete context.

Vocabulary Review Quizzes. These activities provide students with ways to assess their mastery of vocabulary for each act. The quiz items deliberately repeat, in modern language, the context established in the vocabulary in context activities. These quizzes are in a multiple choice format to facilitate evaluation.

EXTENDING ACTIVITIES

Extending activities encourage students to apply what they've learned from studying *Julius Caesar* to alternative situations. Students may complete these activities individually or in groups. This resource includes general directions for extending activities as well as more specific directions for acting out, oral interpretation, using puppet theater, making masks, and writing assignments.

Acting Out

Through improvisations, students can work out a skit to portray a particular scene or place a familiar character in a different context.

Oral Interpretation

These activities encourage students to present scenes from the play in its original language. With the suggested scenes, students can work either individually or in pairs. The directions include steps for preparing an effective oral interpretation. Students may wish to incorporate either puppet theater or masks into their presentations.

Puppet Theater

This activity includes directions for making paper bag puppets and suggestions for two, three, or more performers for specific scenes.

Paper Plate Masks

Masks provide a way to present visual interpretations of a character. Students can do this easily by constructing simple masks from paper plates as shown. These masks, like the puppets, may also be combined with oral or dramatic presentations.

Writing Assignments

Writing tasks give students a chance to incorporate their new understanding of the play into a piece of writing. To develop these assignments, they may want to use some of their reading process activities, such as response journals or character diaries, as sources for prewriting.

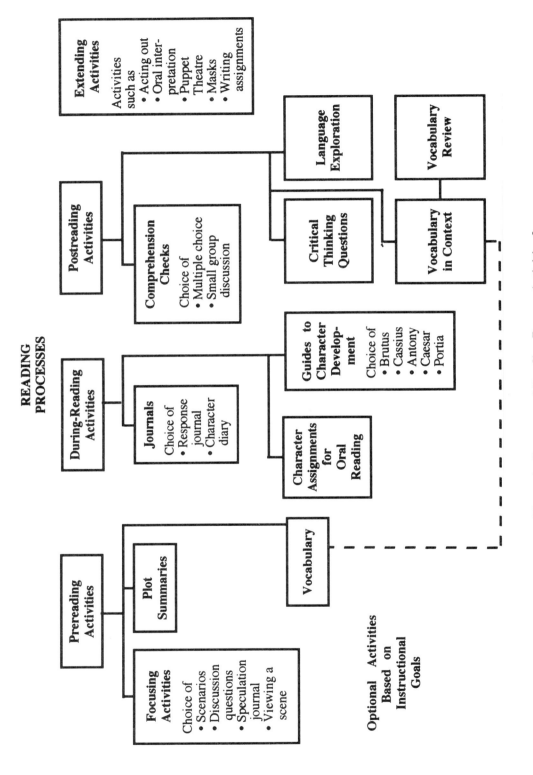

READING PROCESSES

Extending Activities

Activities such as
- Acting out
- Oral inter-pretation
- Puppet Theatre
- Masks
- Writing assignments

Postreading Activities

Comprehension Checks

Choice of
- Multiple choice
- Small group discussion

Language Exploration

Vocabulary Review

Critical Thinking Questions

Vocabulary in Context

During-Reading Activities

Journals

Choice of
- Response journal
- Character diary

Guides to Character Develop-ment

Choice of
- Brutus
- Cassius
- Antony
- Caesar
- Portia

Character Assignments for Oral Reading

Prereading Activities

Plot Summaries

Vocabulary

Focusing Activities

Choice of
- Scenarios
- Discussion questions
- Speculation journal
- Viewing a scene

Optional Activities Based on Instructional Goals

Figure 1: Summary of Reading Process Activities for _Julius Caesar_

PART TWO

INTRODUCTORY MATERIALS
FOR
TEACHING SHAKESPEARE

William Shakespeare

William Shakespeare
April 23, 1564–April 23, 1616

William Shakespeare was the eldest son and third child of John Shakespeare and Mary Arden. His father was a maker of white leather (whittawer) and gloves (glover), and a wool dealer as well as yeoman farmer who owned his own land. As a prosperous and respected tradesman, John Shakespeare also took part in the local government of Stratford and held several government positions including Chamberlain (town treasurer), Alderman (town councilman), and Bailiff of Stratford-upon-Avon.

During William's childhood, Stratford was a prosperous, self-governing market town. As a result, the Corporation of Stratford maintained the grammar school founded originally by the medieval Gild of the Holy Cross where historians believe young William received his early education. The school's gildhall was also where traveling companies of actors most likely performed. Records of the town suggest that William may have seen his first plays during his boyhood. The Chamberlain's accounts show that different companies of traveling players appeared and were paid from the borough's accounts on more than thirty occasions.

Town and church documents also show that William Shakespeare married Ann Hathaway when he was eighteen and she, twenty-six, in 1582. They had three children, Susanna (1583) and twins Hamnet (1585–96) and Judith (1585–1662).

Shortly after his children were born, Shakespeare left Stratford and nothing is known of his life until he began acting in London in 1592. In London, he acted and served as a writer and reviser of plays. At age twenty-eight, he began to impress his contemporaries with the quality and popularity of his work. He published his first narrative poem, *Venus and Adonis* in 1593 and *The Rape of Lucrece* the following year.

While living in London, Shakespeare acted with several companies including the Chamberlain's Men (later called the King's Men) who provided entertainment for the Royal Court. He wrote many of his plays for his own acting company. Shakespeare was also partner in several theatrical ventures including being one of the proprietors of the Globe Theater that was built just outside the city limits of London in 1599. His partners in the Globe also included famous actors of the day—Richard Burbage, Will Kempe, John Heminge, and Henry Condell. Heminge and Condell would publish the first collected editions of Shakespeare's plays, known as the First Folio, in 1623.

Although Shakespeare continued to live and work in London until 1610, he purchased New Place, one of the largest houses in Stratford, in 1597. When he retired to New Place in 1610, he was a wealthy landowner whose estate included farmland, pasture, and gardens. Making occasional visits to London until 1614, Shakespeare continued to associate with actors and playwrights for the rest of his life. While in retirement at Stratford, he surrounded himself with family and friends. Shakespeare died at home on April 23, St. George's Day, in 1616. He was buried in the chancel of Holy Trinity Church in Stratford. He willed New Place to his elder daughter Susanna, then wife of Dr. John Hall. The poet's widow probably lived there with the Halls until her death in 1623. Within a few years of Shakespeare's death, a monument to him was erected and placed on the north wall of Westminster Abbey in London.

An Introduction to Shakespeare's Language

Because Shakespeare wrote nearly four hundred years ago, some of the conventions that he uses in his plays present problems for modern readers. Most of Shakespeare's lines are written in poetry. Although these lines don't usually rhyme, they do have a set rhythm (called *meter).* To achieve the meter, Shakespeare arranges words so that the syllables which are stressed or said more loudly than others fall in a regular pattern: dah DUM dah DUM dah DUM dah DUM dah DUM. For example, read the following lines from *Julius Caesar* aloud:

Yond Cassius has a lean and hungry look;
He thinks too much. Such men are dangerous.

Because you are familiar with the words that Shakespeare uses here, you naturally stressed every second syllable:

yond CAS'sius HAS' a LEAN' and HUN'gry LOOK';
he THINKS' too MUCH'. such MEN'are DAN'ger OUS'.

The pattern of one unstressed syllable followed by a stressed one, dah DUM, is called an *iamb.* Each pattern is referred to as a *foot.* Because Shakespeare uses five iambic feet to a line, this pattern in known as *iambic pentameter.*

In order for Shakespeare to maintain the set meter of most lines, he often structures the lines accordingly. In this way, they differ from what we would consider normal English speech. He may change the order of words so that the stressed syllables fall in the appropriate places. For example, the following sentence has no set meter:

My MAS'ter did BID'me KNEEL' THUS', BRU'tus.

However, Shakespeare turns these words around a bit to maintain the meter in *Julius Caesar:*

ટ્ર

thus BRU'tus, DID' my MAS'ter BID' me KNEEL';

ટ્ર

He may also shorten words by omitting letters so that a two-syllable word is one syllable. As a result, *over* often appears as *o'er* and *'tis* in place of *it is*.

Shakespeare also uses forms of words that we rarely use four hundred years later. Among these are the personal pronouns *thou* (you), *thine* (your, yours), *thee* (you as in "to you"), and *thyself* (yourself). Often Shakespeare also uses verb endings that we no longer do. For example, *hath* is an old form of *has* and *art* an older form of *are*. You are also likely to encounter several words or phrases that we no longer use at all: *anon* instead of *soon* or *shortly,* or *prithee* meaning *I pray to thee (you)*.

Conventions of Shakespeare's Staging

When we attend theatrical performances—school plays, assembly programs, or movies in public theaters—we are accustomed to finding a seat and waiting until the lights dim, the audience quiets down, and the play or feature begins. We're also used to seeing scenery that suggests the location of the play and expect the stage lighting to help set the mood.

But all this was not so in Shakespeare's time. Patrons at that time attended plays during the day, for there was no way to light the stage effectively once the sun had set. Public performance of plays in theaters was a fairly new idea at the time because the first permanent English theater had been built less than twenty years before Shakespeare began writing his plays. Although the shape of the theaters varied from square, circular, or octagonal, all had a stage that was simply a raised platform in an open yard surrounded with tiers of galleries to accommodate the spectators. The stage was covered with a roof, commonly called "The Heavens." While the roof protected the actors from the weather, the attic space above could hold machinery, such as ropes and pulleys to lower thrones or heavenly deities to the stage or to hide the sound effects of thunder, alarum bells, or cannonades. By modern standards these theaters were small. The open yard in front of the stage in one theater measured only fifty-five feet across. Up to two thousand spectators could either sit on benches in the tiers of galleries or stand in the open yard in front of the stage.

These theaters used simple stage props—chairs or tables were brought on the raised platform as needed. Actual scenery may have been suggested through dialogue or may have included minimal set pieces such as a few trees to suggest a forest, or a rock to suggest a river bank. The stages themselves had many built-in acting areas that could function in a number of ways, such as small inner stages with drapes, which the actors used as inner rooms, or raised balconies. The actors could use the inner room for King Duncan's chamber in *Macbeth* or Brutus' tent in *Julius Caesar*. The balcony might serve as Juliet's balcony in *Romeo and Juliet* or as the battlements of Elsinore Castle in *Hamlet*.

The costumes were based on the contemporary clothing styles of the time. Rather than attempt any sort of accurate historical costuming, the actors wore clothes that would suit each character's rank. For example, Macbeth would have been costumed simply as any nobleman and Lady Capulet as a wealthy English merchant's wife. Occasionally, other costume pieces may have been added to suggest witches, fairies, national, or racial costumes.

During the time that Shakespeare wrote and acted, only three or four professional companies performed in theaters just outside the limits of London. These professional troupes employed male actors only. Although many of the roles in Shakespeare's plays are male, the parts of younger female characters—Juliet or her mother, for instance—were played by young boys, aged fourteen or so and apprenticed to actors. Men may have played some female roles, especially those of elder, comedic women like Juliet's Nurse.

Principal Locations for <u>Julius Caesar</u>

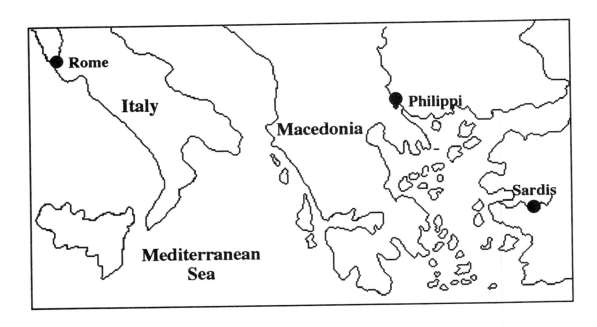

ACT I

Focusing Activities
for
Julius Caesar
Scenarios for Improvisation
Act I

Directions: Presented below are locations and situations involving characters. Before reading an individual scene, pretend to be one of the characters and act out the situation. Don't worry about speaking like characters in Shakespeare's play; just try to imagine how you would react to the situation and use your own language. Take a few minutes to discuss with the other performers what you would like to do. Be prepared to act out your scene for others in the class. Afterward, classmates outside your group may discuss what they've seen.

scene i. *Scene:* A quiet corner of the school cafeteria or commons area before school, at lunch, or immediately after school.

Characters: Pat and Kim.

Situation: Pat tells lifelong friend Kim that she's using and selling crack cocaine. Pat also makes Kim promise not to tell anyone. Improvise the dialogue between them.

scene ii. *Scene:* A public park in Washington, D.C.

Characters: Senators Brook and Clark, two young, idealistic United States Senators.

Situation: Clark has recently been discussed as a possible vice-presidential candidate for the next election. Brook was elected recently because she believes strongly in the principles of representative democracy as stated in the U.S. Constitution. Clark has learned of a movement to abolish the United States House of Representatives and the Senate in favor of allowing the President to remain in office for life. Clark tells Brook that a group of other Senators and Representatives fear the President's increasing power and plan to assassinate the President. For the plan to succeed, Clark needs Brook's help. Improvise the dialogue between them.

**Focusing Activities
for
Julius Caesar
Small Group Discussion Questions
Act I**

Directions: Before reading scenes in Act I, discuss the questions in small groups. You may want to make notes about your discussion, so you can share them with classmates or refer back to them after you've read the scene.

scene i.

1. Based upon what you may have heard or seen, what do you think happens in the play, *Julius Caesar*?

2. What character traits do you feel permit a national leader like the President of the United States to be popular? What character traits do you feel permit a national leader like the President to be effective? What can a national leader do to be both popular and effective?

scene ii.

1. What would a President of the United States have to do that would make you believe that he/she held too much power?

2. Suppose you had learned that there was an extremely popular movement to abolish the House of Representatives and the Senate and to make the current President of the United States King of America. What actions would you be willing to take even though others might consider it treason?

scene iii.

1. Based upon what you've already seen and read in the play, what would make you believe that the ancient Romans were superstitious?

2. What signs or legends do some people use today to predict rain or the length and severity of winter?

Focusing Activities
for
Julius Caesar
Speculation Journal
Act I

Directions: This activity will help you become involved actively with reading the play by helping you to determine a definite purpose for reading. Before you read these scenes in Act I, take a few minutes to respond in writing to the questions below. Don't worry about correct answers here. Use your own experience or what you have read in the play to speculate about what you think will happen. Sometimes, as for scenes i through iii below, you may be asked to speculate about issues that parallel the action of the play. After reading a scene you may find that the characters reacted differently than you thought. Don't worry about these differences; just make note of them because you will have opportunities to share these differences in other activities.

scene i.   Based upon what you have seen or heard, what do you expect *Julius Caesar* to be about?

scene ii.   How would you react if someone suggested that we abolish the U.S. Congress and make the current President of the United States King of America? What would you be willing to do either to support or prevent such a change in government?

scene iii.   What stories, legends, or myths do you know that attempt to explain the occurrence of severe weather or other natural occurrences? What do you think would make people believe these explanations?

After
Reading
Act I:

Now that you have finished reading Act I, which of your speculations were most accurate? How do you account for them? Which ones were least like the action of the play? Why do you think you speculated as you did?

NAME:_____   DATE:_____

Focusing Activity
for
Julius Caesar
Introducing the Play with Videotape

Directions: Before you begin reading *Julius Caesar*, you will view a video version of the first scene. Don't worry about trying to understand everything, just glean a general impression. Note any questions you may want to ask your teacher afterwards. After viewing the scene, take a few minutes to respond to the questions below.

1.   In your own words, describe what you saw briefly. What seems to be the overall conflict or problem in this scene?

2.   Where does this scene take place? Which particular details help you to understand the action?

3.   Based upon what you've seen so far, what kind of person do you expect Julius Caesar to be?

© 1993 by The Center for Applied Research in Education

28

Prereading Activity
for
Julius Caesar
Vocabulary
Act I

Directions: Shakespeare uses the following words in Act I. The section below provides a brief definition of each word and provides a sentence to illustrate its meaning.

Definitions

scene i

1. **battle-ment:** (n.) the upper part of a castle wall with alternating raised and lowered sections from which a battle could be fought.
   Example: During the Middle Ages, soldiers often poured boiling oil from the *battlements* onto the army attacking the castle gate below.

2. **mech-anical:** (n.) a manual worker; a person who performs manual labor. (adj.) pertaining to manual work.
   Example: Carpenters and shoemakers are common types of *mechanical* characters in Shakespeare's plays.

3. **vulgar:** (n. or adj.) the common people; of the common people.
   Example: After the Norman French conquered England, English became the *vulgar* language.

scene ii

4. **barren:** (adj.) unable to bear children or unable to reproduce; sterile.
   Example: The photographs of the moon's surface depict a *barren* landscape.

5. **cogitation:** (n.) thoughts or ideas; the act of thinking or contemplating.
   Example: After a long *cogitation*, Kim developed a useful invention for children: clothes hangers with long necks.

6. **counte-nance:** (n.) appearance, especially of the face.
   Example: From the puppy's *countenance*, we knew she had shredded the newspaper.

29

7. **throng:** (n.) crowd or mob.

   Example: The assembled *throng* of fans surrounded the rock stars completely as they attempted to enter their hotel.

scene iii

8. **conceit** (v.) to think, grasp, or estimate.

   Example: My father's angry tone of voice helped me to *conceit* what he meant by calling me brilliant.

9. **construe:** (v.) to explain or interpret.

   Example: After a while, David could *construe* meaning from Shakespeare's words.

10. **ordinance:** (n.) normal or usual placement of things in the world; natural order.

    Example: In over forty years, nothing has disturbed the normal *ordinance* of Grandma's living room.

Prereading Activity
for
Julius Caesar
Plot Summaries
Act I

Directions: To help you better understand and follow Shakespeare's play, read the summary of specific scenes immediately before you begin to read the original. If you get lost during the scene, refer to the summary again.

Act I, scene i

Flavius and Marullus, two tribunes who are the elected representatives of the people of Rome, meet a carpenter and cobbler in the streets. The tribunes ask the citizens why they have taken the day off from work. They reply that Caesar is returning after defeating Pompey's sons. Flavius and Marullus scold the citizens and remind them that they once also celebrated Pompey's return. Flavius and Marullus then decide to remove the scarves that decorate the statues of Caesar throughout the city.

Act I, scene ii

During the foot race to celebrate the Feast of Lupercal, Caesar directs his wife Calphurnia to stand close to the race course, so that Mark Antony can touch her and cure her barrenness. The Soothsayer warns Caesar to beware the Ides of March (March 15).

Cassius asks Brutus to explain what has been bothering him lately. Brutus, who is at first reluctant to reveal his concerns, admits finally that he's afraid the people of Rome will make Caesar their king. If Caesar becomes king, the Roman Republic will come to an end. Cassius points out how human Caesar is. First, Cassius tells how he saved Caesar from drowning once, saw Caesar catch a fever, and witnessed one of Caesar's epileptic seizures. They hear the crowds cheer three times. Cassius then points out that Brutus is as honorable a man as Caesar, but Caesar is gaining power. Brutus promises to think about what Cassius has said and discuss it with him further at a later time.

Caesar admits he doesn't trust Cassius, for he "thinks too much" and doesn't show his thoughts or feelings openly. Casca then tells Brutus and Cassius how Caesar has declined the crown three times. They also learn that Caesar had another seizure and that Caesar has had Marullus and Flavius killed for removing the decorations from Caesar's statues.

Once Cassius is alone, he comments that although Brutus is Caesar's friend, he may be ready to change.

Act I,
scene iii

The same evening Casca and Cicero meet during a violent thunderstorm. Although Cicero sees the storm as wonderful, Casca describes the frightening omens he has seen since he escorted Caesar home. Casca has never seen a storm that dropped fire until tonight. Casca saw a slave hold up his hand, have it catch fire, yet not be burned. When Casca passed the Capitol, he met a lion that ignored him. A group of women claimed to have seen men "all in fire" walking the streets. Finally, he adds that an owl (the bird of night) was seen in the market at noon.

Cicero asks if Caesar will come to the Senate the next day. Casca replies that Antony has planned to send for Caesar.

Casca then meets Cassius. Cassius has dared the storm to strike him and been spared. Cassius suggests that the world is out of order because an ordinary man (Caesar) has grown too powerful. Even Casca can guess that Cassius means Caesar, whom the Senate plans to name king the next day. Cassius, who opposes giving up the representative republic form of government to Caesar, suggests that his dagger will keep Cassius a free man. Casca also vows to fight to retain his freedom. Cassius then convinces Casca that Caesar is a tyrant and enlists Casca's support.

When Cassius meets Cinna, Cassius promises to get Brutus' support for the plot against Caesar. Cassius instructs Cinna to take a note to Brutus and then meet him and the other conspirators at Pompey's theater. Cassius and Casca promise to meet the others after they've spoken with Brutus.

© 1993 by The Center for Applied Research in Education

Class Period:

CHARACTER ASSIGNMENTS FOR ORAL READING GROUPS

Julius Caesar

Session 1: Act I

Characters	*Group 1*	*Group 2*	*Group 3*	*Group 4*
Marullus, Cinna	___	___	___	___
Flavius, Soothsayer, Calphurnia	___	___	___	___
First Citizen (carpenter), Casca	___	___	___	___
Second Citizen (cobbler), Cicero	___	___	___	___
Caesar	___	___	___	___
Antony	___	___	___	___
Brutus	___	___	___	___
Cassius	___	___	___	___

33

**During-reading Activity
for
Julius Caesar
*Directions for Response Journal***

Although we often read silently, reading is an active process. As we run our eyes across a line of text, we transform the letters and words into mental images. The words have the power to affect us in many ways. This response journal will help you state several different types of responses immediately after you've read and assist you in recalling the experiences of reading before discussing it with your classmates.

Your response journal is a place for you to react personally to what you read. This is a place to begin piecing together your understanding of the play. Your journal is a place to think aloud on paper and not have to worry about grammatical correctness or punctuation. You may want to do this as you read or immediately upon finishing a reading session. It won't be nearly as effective if you put it off! There are four types of responses you should attempt each time. None of these needs to be more than a brief paragraph.

1. *Respond emotionally.* How does the play make you feel at this point? Record your emotions in a few sentences and then try to figure out why you feel as you do.

2. *Make associations between ideas in the text and your personal experience.* In what situations have you felt like the characters? What persons, places, or ideas from your own experiences came to your mind while you were reading this portion of the play? List three to five associations, but don't worry about why they came to mind. Just accept that they occur.

3. *Look at the language.* What portions of Shakespeare's language attracts your attention? These might be individual words, phrases, lines, scenes, or images. Make note of whatever feature(s) draw your attention. Speculate for a few minutes about what you think these might mean.

4. *Record any questions or problems.* Make note of any portion of the play, its language, or events that seemed to cause you problems. Write down any questions that occur to you as you read.

Here's a sample journal for Act I, scene i:

1. Those official guys, Marullus and Flavius, sure do think they're better than the working guys. They really talk down to them and treat them like they're stupid. They're just normal working guys who learn of this guy Caesar's big parade into the city and want to go to watch. It's like cheering the local college or pro team that wins a national title.

2. Reminds me of the principal stopping kids in the hall who are enjoying themselves.
   Fans cheering at a game.
   The shoemaker's jokes remind me of kids' riddles.

3. The second citizen's (shoemaker) line: "A trade sir, that I hope I may use with a safe conscience; which is indeed sir, a mender of bad soles." I get the joke: soles and souls.

4. Is the Pompey in this scene a person or the place that got wiped out by the volcano?

During-reading Activity
for
Julius Caesar
Response Journal

Directions: Use the spaces below to record your responses to the acts and scenes of *Julius Caesar* that you've just finished reading. Respond in all four ways and take a few additional minutes to explore why you responded as you did.

Response Journal for Act ___, scene ____ to Act ____, scene ___.

1. How does the play make you feel at this point? Record your emotional response(s) in a few sentences and then explore them for a few minutes, trying to figure out why you feel as you do.

2. In what situations have you felt similar to the characters? What persons, places, or ideas from your own experiences came to your mind while you were reading this portion of the play? Try to list at least three associations, but don't worry about why they came to mind. Just accept that they occur.

    a.

    b.

    c.

3. What portions of Shakespeare's language attracts your attention? These might be individual words, phrases, lines, scenes, or images. Make note of whatever feature(s) draw your attention. Speculate for a few minutes about what you think these might mean.

4. Make note of any portion of the play, its language, or events that seem to cause you problems. Note any questions that you might ask.

During-reading Activity
for
Julius Caesar
Directions for Character Diary

As you read *Julius Caesar*, you will find that the events of the play affect the lives of some twenty characters, not just the lives of one. To give you an opportunity to explore the reactions of other characters, pretend to be one of the characters. For this assignment, keep the personal diary of a single character for the one week during which the play takes place.

Select one of the following characters for your diary:

Octavius Caesar, Julius Caesar's nephew, later Emperor Augustus	Mark Antony
Calphurnia, wife of Julius Caesar	Marcus Brutus
Cassius	Casca
Artemidorus	Soothsayer
Lucius, Brutus' servant	Pindarus, Cassius' Servant
Portia, wife of Marcus Brutus	

In your diary, summarize the events of the act and provide an explanation for how your character may have heard of them, if the character was not involved in the events directly, and react as your character would. For example, Calphurnia appears only in Act I, scene ii, and again in Act II, scene ii. However, because she survives Caesar's assassination, she would logically become a part of Octavius' household and come under his protection. It's not too farfetched to think that Octavius might correspond either with her or with other members of his household. Part of her diary for Act I (March 14, 44 B.C.) might look like this:

March 14

What a wonderful day this has been for Julius! He returned triumphant to Rome after defeating the sons of Pompey. He chose today to reenter the city because it was also the Feast of Lupercal.

During the great foot race, I did as Julius commanded and stood close enough to the runners so that Mark Antony could touch me and cure my barrenness. I wish I could give Julius a son and heir. After the race, Mark Antony did encourage the people to make Julius their king. Three times did Antony offer him the crown and three times did he refuse it. He says instead that the Senate may give him the crown tomorrow.

After such a wonderful day, we now are having a terrible storm with lightning and thunder like I have never seen before.

Use the following summary of events to help you keep your character diary for *Julius Caesar:*

Acts and scenes	*Time, Place and Approximate Date*
Act I, scenes i and ii	Rome 44 B.C., March 14 the afternoon
scene iii	That evening
Act II, scene i	Early in the morning March 15 (the Ides of March)
scenes ii and iii	Morning, March 15
Act III, scenes i–iii	Later that day, March 15, 44 B.C.
Act IV, scene i	A few days or months after the assassination
scenes ii and iii	Many months later, possibly 43 B.C.
Act V, scenes i–v	Many more months later, 42 B.C.

NAME:_____ DATE:_____

During-reading Activity
for
Julius Caesar
Character Diary 1
Act I, scenes i, ii, iii

Directions: Use the space below to record your character's reactions to the events that occur in Act I in *Julius Caesar*. Remember to include a summary of events, explain how your character learned of them, and give your character's reactions to these events. Because the act contains three scenes, you may wish to record your character's entries as you read each scene. If you need additional room, use the back of this sheet.

The Personal Diary of

_____
(character's name)

Rome
March 14, 44 B.C.

_____

_____

_____

_____

_____

_____

_____

_____

_____

_____

_____

_____

_____

_____

_____

_____

© 1993 by The Center for Applied Research in Education

NAME:_____   DATE:_____

During-reading Activity
for
Julius Caesar
Viewing Act I, scene ii
Brutus and Cassius' First Meeting

Directions: After you've read this scene from *Julius Caesar*, viewing a film or video version may help you better understand how the text translates into characters' actions. Although you may want to keep your copy of the play handy, don't be surprised if the actors' script varies some from yours. Film scripts often delete or reorder the lines of the play. You may want to note questions to ask your teacher afterwards. After viewing the scene, take a few minutes to respond to the questions below.

1. What do the costumes and the set representing the Roman street tell you about Rome during the time of the play?

2. What seems to be Brutus' attitude towards Caesar during this scene? What seems to motivate Brutus and how does it contrast with what seems to motivate Cassius? How do the actors' facial expressions, tones of voice, and gestures enhance Shakespeare's words?

3. At this point in the play, what seems to be the nature of the relationship between Brutus and Cassius?

NAME:_____   DATE:_____

During-reading Activity
for
Julius Caesar
Guide to Character Development: Brutus
Act I

Shakespeare reveals his characters in four ways:

๛ through what the characters say to other characters in dialogue

๛ through what the characters reveal about their thoughts through long speeches to the audience called *soliloquies*

๛ through what other characters say about them

๛ through what they do, their actions

As you read the play, examine the following scenes for what they reveal about Brutus' character and fill in the chart briefly using your own words. If you need more room, use the back of the page.

Scene	What Brutus says, does, or what others say about him	What this reveals about Brutus' character
Act I, scene ii Brutus first talks with Cassius		
Act I, scene iii Cinna and Cassius discuss Brutus		

© 1993 by The Center for Applied Research in Education

NAME:_____   DATE:_____

During-reading Activity
for
Julius Caesar
Guide to Character Development: Cassius
Act I

Shakespeare reveals his characters in four ways:

- through what the characters say to other characters in dialogue
- through what the characters reveal about their thoughts through long speeches to the audience called *soliloquies*
- through what other characters say about them
- through what they do, their actions

As you read the play, examine the following scenes for what they reveal about Cassius' character and fill in the chart briefly using your own words. If you need more room, use the back of the page.

Scene	What Cassius says, does, or what others say about him	What this reveals about Cassius' character
Act I, scene ii Cassius and Brutus meet		
Act I, scene iii Cinna and Cassius discuss Caesar		

During-reading Activity
for
Julius Caesar
Guide to Character Development: Antony
Act I

Shakespeare reveals his characters in four ways:

- through what the characters say to other characters in dialogue
- through what the characters reveal about their thoughts through long speeches to the audience called *soliloquies*
- through what other characters say about them
- through what they do, their actions

As you read the play, examine the following scenes for what they reveal about Antony's character and fill in the chart briefly using your own words. If you need more room, use the back of the page.

Scene	What Antony says, does, or what others say about him	What this reveals about Antony's character
Act I, scene ii Antony attends Caesar		

During-reading Activity
for
Julius Caesar
Guide to Character Development: Caesar
Act I

Shakespeare reveals his characters in four ways:

- through what the characters say to other characters in dialogue
- through what the characters reveal about their thoughts through long speeches to the audience called *soliloquies*
- through what other characters say about them
- through what they do, their actions

As you read the play, examine the following scenes for what they reveal about Caesar's character and fill in the chart briefly using your own words. If you need more room, use the back of the page.

Scene	What Caesar says, does, or what others say about him	What this reveals about Caesar's character
Act I, scene i Marullus and Flavius admonish the citizens and take down scarves from Caesar's statues		
Act I, scene ii Caesar instructs Antony and refuses the crown		
Act I, scene iii Cassius and Casca discuss Caesar		

Postreading Activity
for
Julius Caesar
Comprehension Check
Act I

Directions: After you've read all of Act I, use the following questions to check how well you've understood what you've read. For each question, select the most appropriate answer from the choices listed below it. Place the letter corresponding to your answer in the space to the left of the item number.

_____1. At the end of scene i, what do Marullus and Flavius go to do?

   A. Make the citizens return to work.
   B. Kill Caesar.
   C. Start a riot against Caesar.
   D. Remove scarves from Caesar's statues.
   E. Celebrate the Festival of Lupercal.

_____2. When Cassius and Brutus discuss Caesar in scene ii, Cassius tells Brutus all of the following except that

   A. Cassius was born free.
   B. Caesar has been named king.
   C. Cassius saved Caesar from drowning.
   D. Caesar has fits.
   E. Caesar can catch fevers.

_____3. When Caesar says,

                              ❧

            Yond Cassius has a lean and hungry look;
            He thinks too much. Such men are dangerous.

                              ❧

he suggests that Cassius

   A. is malnourished.
   B. has an outgoing personality.
   C. is pensive and brooding.
   D. is the life of any party.
   E. is powerful.

_____4. For Cicero, the storm in scene iii is

      A. something wonderful to see.
      B. something to be terrified of.
      C. something to foretell his own future with.
      D. an omen of Caesar's death.
      E. an omen of Casca's death.

_____5. What person is Cassius referring to in these lines to Casca?

ᴥ

Now could I, Casca, name thee a man,
Most like this dreadful night,
That thunders, lightens, opens graves, and roars
As doth the lion in the Capitol;
A man no mightier than thyself, or me,
In personal action; yet prodigious grown,
And fearful, as these strange eruptions are.

ᴥ

      A. Brutus
      B. Himself
      C. Antony
      D. Caesar
      E. Octavius

Postreading Activity
for
Julius Caesar
Small Group Discussion to Check Comprehension
Act I

Directions: After you've read all of Act I, in small groups, discuss each of the following questions briefly. Use the space below each question to note points you may wish to share later. If you need more room, use the back of the page.

1. What makes Julius Caesar appealing to the common citizens of Rome but so unappealing to elected officials like Marullus and Flavius?

2. In scene ii, how does Caesar's refusal of the crown make him even more popular with the people of Rome?

3. Why is Caesar suspicious of Cassius?

4. In scene ii, what does Cassius point out to Brutus that makes Brutus even more suspicious of Caesar's power?

5. In scene iii, how does Cicero's interpretation of the strange storm contrast with that of Casca?

NAME:_____   DATE:_____

Postreading Activity
for
Julius Caesar
Critical Thinking Questions
Act I

Directions: To help develop your understanding of Act I, take time to think about and discuss these questions. The first question is the focus question and the point of the discussion. Don't be concerned that you may not be able to answer it at first. Proceed to the exploration questions and then return to the focus question.

Focus Question. Under what circumstances does it become necessary for an individual, like Brutus, to break the law?

Exploration Questions.

1. Under what circumstances would you reveal a friend's secret to a parent, teacher, or other person of authority?

2. Although Brutus and Cassius both plot to assassinate Caesar, in what ways do you think their motives differ?

3. As forms of government, what are the advantages and disadvantages of governing by one person, as in a monarchy or dictatorship, over governing by a group, as in a representative democracy like the United States or Great Britain?

4. To which of Brutus' ideals does Cassius need to appeal to convince Brutus to betray his friend Caesar?

5. Aside from what Brutus, Cassius, and the other conspirators do and say, what other evidence does Shakespeare provide in Act I to imply that Caesar does not have universal support among all Romans?

6. What would you do if you learned that most of the members of the U.S. Congress were in favor of eliminating our form of democratic government in favor of making our current President the King of America?

Postreading Activity
for
Julius Caesar
Language Exploration
Review of Figurative Language
Act I

As other poets and playwrights do, Shakespeare also explores such abstract ideas as justice, personal honor, and sacrificing the good of the individual for the good of all in his plays. He often connects abstract ideas with concrete examples through *figurative language.* Although we rarely mean figurative language in a literal sense, it does help us express our ideas more vividly. Common language devices associated with figurative language include *simile, metaphor, personification, and apostrophe.*

A *simile* compares two different terms using *like* or *as.* In daily speech we often use similes like these:

&

Sam is as hungry as a bear.
Angel runs like the wind.

&

Another way to compare two different terms is to use a *metaphor.* Unlike a simile, a metaphor makes a comparison directly without using *like* or *as.* As metaphors, the previous examples look like this:

&

Sam is a real bear when he's hungry.
Angel breezed across the finish line.

&

We also use *personification* to give human characteristics to inanimate or non-human things. We may say that "Love is blind," or argue with the soft drink machine that "eats" our change.

A fourth figurative device is to address a person or abstract idea that is not or cannot be present. This device is called *apostrophe.* Note the following examples:

&

Death, be not proud.
Twinkle, twinkle little star,
How I wonder what you are?

&

Directions: The following passages contain examples of simile, metaphor, personification, and apostrophe. Working in pairs, small groups, or as your teacher directs, identify each figurative device and then review each passage within the context of the play to decide what it suggests to the reader.

1. Marullus speaking to the citizens (scene i):

ﻉ

Many a time and oft
Have you climbed up to walls and battlements,
. . .

To see great Pompey pass the streets of Rome.
And when you saw his chariot appear,
Have you not made an universal shout,
That Tiber trembled underneath her banks . . .

ﻉ

2. Flavius commenting to Marullus before leaving to remove the scarves from Caesar's statues (scene i):

ﻉ

These growing feathers plucked from Caesar's wing
Will make him fly an ordinary pitch,
Who else would soar above the view of men,
And keep us all in servile fearfulness.

ﻉ

3.   Cassius to Brutus (scene ii):

&

And since you know you cannot see yourself
So well as by reflection, I your glass,
Will modestly discover to yourself
That of yourself which you yet know not of.

&

4.   Cassius describing his rescue of Caesar from drowning (scene ii):

&

I, as Aeneas, our great ancestor,
Did from the flames of Troy upon his shoulder
The old Anchises bear, so from the waves of Tiber
Did I the tired Caesar.

&

5.   Cassius commenting on his discussion with Brutus (scene ii):

&

Well Brutus, thou art noble; yet I see
Thy honorable mettle may be wrought
From that it is disposed.

&

6. Casca to Cicero (scene iii):

ະ

A common slave—you know him well by sight—
Held up his left hand, which did flame and burn
Like twenty torches joined;

ະ

7. Cassius to Casca (scene iii):

ະ

Now could I, Casca, name thee a man,
Most like this dreadful night,

ະ

8. Cassius to Casca (scene iii):

ະ

Therein, ye gods, you make the weak most strong;
Therein, ye gods, you tyrants do defeat.

ະ

9.   Cassius to Casca (scene iii):

≈

But life, being weary of these worldly bars,
Never lacks power to dismiss itself.

≈

10.   Cassius to Casca (scene iii):

≈

And why should Caesar be a tyrant then?
Poor man, I know he would not be a wolf,
But that he sees the Romans are but sheep;

≈

NAME:_____ **DATE:**_____

Postreading Activity
for
Julius Caesar
Vocabulary in Context
Act I

Directions: In each of the passages below you will find one of the words from the prereading vocabulary list for Act I. Review the definitions given in the prereading vocabulary. Working individually, in pairs, or in small groups as your teacher directs, examine each of the underlined words in the following passages from Act I. For each word, use the appropriate meaning and develop a brief interpretation of the passage within the context of the play.

1. Flavius (scene i) to the working men:

❧

What, know you not,
Being <u>mechanical</u>, you ought not walk
Upon a laboring day without the sign
Of your profession?

❧

2. Marullus (scene i) speaking to the Citizens:

❧

Many a time and oft,
Have you climbed up to walls and <u>battlements</u>,
To towers and windows, yea, to chimney tops,
Your infants in your arms, and there have sat
. . .
To see great Pompey pass the streets of Rome.

❧

© 1993 by The Center for Applied Research in Education

3. Flavius (scene i) asking Marullus to help him disperse the crowds:

    &

    I'll about
    And drive away the vulgar from the streets.

    &

4. Caesar to Antony (scene ii):

    &

    . . . for our elders say,
    The barren, touched in this holy chase,
    Shake off their sterile curse.

    &

5. Caesar to the Soothsayer (scene ii):

    &

    Fellow, come from the throng, look upon Caesar.

    &

6. Brutus to Cassius (scene ii):

    &

    I turn the trouble of my countenance
    Merely upon myself.

    &

© 1993 by The Center for Applied Research in Education

7.   Cassius to Brutus (scene ii):

ا‌ﻪ

By means where of this breast of mine hath buried
Thoughts of great value, worthy <u>cogitations</u>.

ا‌ﻪ

8.   Cicero to Casca (scene iii):

ا‌ﻪ

Indeed, it is a strange-disposed time.
But men may <u>construe</u> things after their fashion.

ا‌ﻪ

9.   Cassius to Casca (scene iii):

ا‌ﻪ

Why all these things change from their <u>ordinance</u>.

ا‌ﻪ

10.   Cassius to Casca and Cinna (scene iii):

ا‌ﻪ

Him, and his worth, and our great need of him,
You have right well <u>conceited</u>.

ا‌ﻪ

Vocabulary Review Quiz
for
Julius Caesar
Act I

Directions: For each of the italicized words in the sentences below, determine which letter best reflects the use of the word in this context. Place the letter corresponding to your answer in the space to the left of the item number.

1. Flavius and Marullus remind the citizens that they are *mechanical* characters.
   In this context, *mechanical* means

   A. dealing with machines   B. absent minded   C. manual laborers
   D. machines

2. According to Marullus, the peasants of Rome once climbed chimneys and *battlements* to view Pompey as he entered in triumph.
   In this context, *battlement* means

   A. roof   B. upper part of castle wall   C. valley   D. fight

3. The tribunes wanted to clear the *vulgar* from the streets.
   In this context, *vulgar* means

   A. common people   B. profaners   C. foul-mouthed   D. immoral

4. Caesar's wife, Calphurnia, is *barren*.
   In this context, *barren* means

   A. especially beautiful   B. boring   C. sterile   D. pregnant

5. Cassius often refers to his *cogitations* as reasons for having to assassinate Caesar.
   In this context, *cogitation* means

   A. excitement   B. boredom   C. periods of thought   D. knowledge

6. Caesar tells the Soothsayer to come from the *throng*.
   In this context, *throng* means

   A. crowd   B. sandal   C. raised platform   D. shadows

7. Brutus sees his own problems in his own *countenance*.
   In this context, *countenance* means

   A. numbering device   B. counsel   C. facial appearance
   D. surroundings

© 1993 by The Center for Applied Research in Education

8. Cassius praises Casca and Cinna for their ability to *conceit*.
    In this context, *conceit* means

    A. evaluate themselves highly   B. estimate   C. create   **D. destroy**

9. Cicero comments upon humankind's desire to observe the **world and**
    construe meaning.
    In this context, *construe* means

    A. destroy   B. build   C. misunderstand   D. interpret

10. The Elizabethans believed in the specific *ordinance* of **the world.**
    In this context, *ordinance* means

    A. natural order   B. displacement   C. ammunition   **D. appearance**

ACT II

Focusing Activities
for
Julius Caesar
Scenarios for Improvisation
Act II

Directions: Presented below are locations and situations involving characters. Before reading an individual scene, pretend to be one of the characters and act out the situation. Don't worry about speaking like characters in Shakespeare's play; just try to imagine how you would react to the situation and use your own language. Take a few minutes to discuss with the other performers what you would like to do. Be prepared to act out your scene for others in the class. Afterward, classmates outside your group may discuss what they've seen.

scene i. *Scene:* The garden of Brutus' house.

Characters: Brutus and Cassius.

Situation: Brutus, who has been Caesar's lifelong friend, fears Caesar's increasing power and the possibility of his becoming king. Cassius feels Caesar is already too powerful and must be stopped. For Cassius' plan to succeed, he needs Brutus' help. Improvise the dialogue between them.

scene ii. *Scene:* The living room of Jamie's house.

Characters: Leslie and Jamie.

Situation: Leslie and Jamie have been planning this evening for weeks. Leslie has just gotten a driver's license and tonight is the first time Leslie has the use of her family car. Last night Jamie had a nightmare, dreaming that the two of them had been killed in a terrible accident. Leslie is picking up Jamie and wants to go out as planned. As a result of the dream, Jamie doesn't. Improvise the dialogue between them.

scene iv. *Scene:* Brutus' garden after Cassius, the other conspirators, and Ligarius have left.

Characters: Brutus and Portia.

Situation: Portia has noticed that Brutus has been troubled lately. He hasn't eaten or slept for days. Brutus has decided to join the conspiracy to murder Caesar. Portia reminds Brutus of his earlier promise to tell her what was on his mind. Improvise the dialogue between them.

**Focusing Activities
for
Julius Caesar
Small Group Discussion Questions
*Act II***

Directions: Before reading scenes in Act II, discuss the questions in small groups. You may wish to make notes about your discussion, so you can share them with classmates or refer back to them after you've read the scene.

scene i.

1. Based upon what you have seen of Brutus' character in Act I, what do you think he will tell Cassius when they meet again?

2. Now that you've seen Cassius discuss the plot against Caesar with both Brutus and Casca in Act I, what means do you think Cassius might employ to convince Brutus to join the conspiracy?

scene ii.

1. From what you've seen of Caesar's character in Act I, scene ii, what means do you think the conspirators might employ to convince Caesar to go to the Senate?

2. Casca and Cicero discuss the strange storm in Act I, scene iii. This same storm continues throughout the night in Act II, scene i. From what you've seen of both Caesar's and Calphurnia's characters, how would you expect each to react to the storm?

scenes iii
and iv.

1. If you were to learn of the conspiracy against Caesar, how might you attempt to warn him?

2. Based upon what you've seen of the relationship between Brutus and his wife Portia, why do you believe that Brutus would (or wouldn't) tell her about joining the conspiracy against Caesar?

Focusing Activities
for
Julius Caesar
Speculation Journal
Act II

Directions: This activity will help you become involved actively with reading the play by helping you to determine a definite purpose for reading. Before you read these scenes in Act II, take a few minutes to respond in writing to the questions below. Don't worry about correct answers here. Use your own experience or what you have read in the play to speculate about what you think will happen. After reading a scene you may find that the characters reacted differently than you thought. Don't worry about these differences; just make note of them because you will have opportunities to share these differences in other activities.

scene i. Based upon what you have already seen of Brutus' character in Act I, what answer do you think Brutus will give to Cassius and the others about Julius Caesar's increasing power? What do you think they plan to do about it?

scene ii. Based upon what you've seen of the characters of Julius Caesar and his wife Calphurnia in Act I, scene ii, what do you think the conspirators might need to do to ensure Caesar's presence at the Senate? What do you think Calphurnia might do to prevent him from going?

scene iii. If you were to learn of the conspiracy against Caesar, what would you need to do to warn him?

scene iv. Based upon what you've seen of the relationship between Brutus and his wife Portia at the end of Act II, scene i, why do you think Brutus would (or wouldn't) tell her of his plans and how do you think she will react to them?

**After
Reading
Act II:**

Now that you have finished reading the act, which of your speculations were most accurate? How do you account for them? Which ones were least like the action of the play? Why do you think you speculated as you did?

Prereading Activity
for
Julius Ceasar
Vocabulary
Act II

Directions: Shakespeare uses the following words in Act II. The section below provides a sentence to illustrate its meaning.

Definitions.

scene i

1. **betwixt:**   (prep. or adv.) an archaic form of *between.*
   Example: Teenagers are *betwixt* twelve and twenty.

2. **extrem-
   ities:**   (n.) condition or state of extreme need.
   Example: The *extremities* of the prolonged drought caused the American charities to airlift food and medicine to Ethiopia.

3. **faction:**   (n.) a political party or group; set of conspirators, intrigue.
   Example: In large cities, large gangs often create rival *factions* within themselves.

4. **wary:**   (adj.) careful, watchful; on one's guard.
   Example: Walking alone at night, Steve was *wary* of strangers.

scene ii

5. **imminent:** (adj.) threatening, perilous.
   Example: The hurricane warning suggested *imminent* catastrophe for the coastal communities.

6. **prevail:**   (v.) to prove superior in power or influence; to win out.
   Example: Believing in her son's innocence, the mother *prevailed* and had him reinstated as president of the company.

7. **thrice:**   (adv.) three times.
   Example: Anthony failed his driver's test *thrice* but got his license on the fourth try.

8. **valiant**:   (adj.) brave, courageous.
   Example: The firefighters made a *valiant* effort to control the blaze.

scene iii

9. **contrive:** (v.) to conspire; to invent.
    Example: The witnesses' stories were so bizarre that the jury thought they *contrived* them to help the defendant.

scene iv

10. **fray:** (n.) a noisy quarrel.
    Example: When a fight broke out at the baseball game, the umpires and coaches waded into the *fray* to stop it.

Prereading Activity
for
Julius Caesar
Plot Summaries
Act II

Directions: To help you better understand and follow Shakespeare's play, read the summary of specific scenes immediately before you begin to read the original. If you get lost during the scene, refer to the summary again.

Act II, Brutus sends his servant Lucius to light the lamp in his study. Alone
scene i in his garden, he realizes that the only way to control Caesar is to kill him. Although Brutus has no personal reason to kill his friend, Brutus realizes Caesar's nature might change for the worst if he were to become king. He believes the only way to prevent Caesar from becoming a tyrannical king is to kill him before he can be crowned.

After lighting a lamp, Lucius returns with Cassius' letter for Brutus. Lucius cannot recall putting the letter in the window. Brutus takes the letter and asks Lucius to check the calendar to see if tomorrow is the Ides of March.

The storm is so bright that Brutus reads the letter that urges him to wake up and redress the wrongs of Rome. Cassius, along with Casca, Decius, Cinna, Metellus Cimber, and Trebonius, come to see Brutus. After Cassius takes Brutus aside, Cassius asks all to take an oath. Brutus argues that they need no secret oath for their cause is just.

As the group considers others that they might enlist for support, Brutus argues against including them. Cicero will not join anything that he did not begin. Cassius urges the conspirators to kill Antony also, but Brutus argues to leave Antony out because the plot will seem too bloody.

Cassius points out that Caesar has become more suspicious lately and may not come to the Senate. They all agree to accompany Caesar, whom they believe will not be able to refuse all of them. At dawn, they leave; Brutus warns the conspirators not to let their faces betray the plan.

Portia, Brutus' wife, comes to ask what is troubling him. He has not slept, talked, or eaten since the day before. Brutus tries to pass it all off with a simple "I'm not well." Portia knows that if he weren't well he would seek help. She knows that something he is thinking about is the trouble and, as his wife, he needs to share it with her. He promises to tell her soon. Caius Ligarius, who has risen from his sick bed to join Brutus and the others, arrives.

© 1993 by The Center for Applied Research in Education

Act II, scene ii

Meanwhile, the storm continues and disrupts Caesar's house as well. During the night, Caesar's wife Calphurnia has called out in a dream that Caesar has been murdered. Caesar sends a servant to make a sacrifice and let him know if the priests feel it is successful in appeasing the gods.

Caesar, who has always faced his fears, is determined to go to the Senate today. Calphurnia urges Caesar to stay home because of evil omens she and others have seen. A lioness gave birth in the streets; graves have come open; the strange storm has dropped fire; blood has dripped from the Capitol. Caesar, however, points out that fate cannot be avoided. Calphurnia begs Caesar to send Antony to the Senate in his place.

When Decius comes for Caesar, Caesar tells Decius to inform the senators that he will not come today. Although Calphurnia urges Decius to say her husband is ill, Caesar insists that he owes the Senate no explanation but explains privately that Calphurnia wishes him to stay home because of her dream. In the dream, Caesar's statue spouted blood and many Romans came and bathed their hands in it. Decius offers a flattering interpretation: Caesar's blood will revive Rome. Once Caesar is crowned, many Romans will come to seek advice and wisdom from Caesar. Decius then tells Caesar that the Senate indeed plans to offer the crown to him today and that he must be there to receive it. Caesar decides to go with the others when they come for him.

Act II, scene iii

Outside Caesar's house, Artemidorus reads a letter warning Caesar about Brutus and vows to give it to Caesar as he passes.

Act II, scene iv

Outside Brutus' house, Portia is worried about Brutus because she knows of his plans. She asks Lucius to run to the Senate and check on Brutus. She thinks she hears noises but Lucius hears none. As the Soothsayer passes, Portia asks if he has seen Caesar yet. The Soothsayer says no, but that he has to see Caesar before he goes to the Senate. The Soothsayer leaves to find Caesar elsewhere because the narrowness of the street in front of Brutus' house could cause the crows to crush him.

Class Period:

CHARACTER ASSIGNMENTS FOR ORAL READING GROUPS

Julius Caesar

Session 2: Act II

Characters	*Group 1*	*Group 2*	*Group 3*	*Group 4*
Brutus	____	____	____	____
Lucius, Casca, Antony	____	____	____	____
Cassius, Ligarius	____	____	____	____
Cinna, Caesar	____	____	____	____
Metellus, Caesar's servant, Soothsayer	____	____	____	____
Decius	____	____	____	____
Trebonius, Calphurnia, Publius	____	____	____	____
Portia, Artemidorus	____	____	____	____

72

NAME:_____   DATE:_____

During-reading Activity
for
Julius Caesar
Character Diary 2
Act II, scenes i, ii, iii, and iv

Directions: Use the space below to record your character's reactions to the events that occur in Act II in *Julius Caesar*. Remember to include a summary of events, explain how your character learned of them, and give your character's reactions to these events. Because the act contains three scenes, you may wish to record your character's entries as you read each scene. If you need additional room, use the back of this sheet.

The Personal Diary of

_____
(character's name)

Rome
March 15, 44 B.C.
Morning

_____

_____

_____

_____

_____

_____

_____

_____

_____

_____

_____

_____

_____

_____

_____

NAME:_____ DATE:_____

During-reading Activity
for
Julius Caesar
Viewing Act II, scene i
Brutus Joins the Conspiracy

Directions: Read this scene before viewing a video of it. Viewing the film or video version should help you to better understand how the text translates into characters' motives and actions. Although you may want to keep your copy of the play handy, don't be surprised if the actors' script varies from yours. Film scripts often delete or reorder the lines of the plays. You may want to note questions to ask after you have seen the video. After viewing the scene, take a few minutes to respond to the questions below.

1. What do the costumes, the set representing Brutus' house and garden, and the stage properties (like the furnishings and household objects) tell you about Brutus' position as a Senator?

2. What seems to be Brutus' attitude towards Caesar during this scene? What seems to motivate Brutus and how does it contrast with what seems to motivate Cassius? How do the actors' facial expressions, tones of voice, and gestures enhance Shakespeare's words?

3. What seems to be the nature of the relationship between Brutus and Portia?

During-reading Activity
for
Julius Caesar
Guide to Character Development: Brutus
Act II

Shakespeare reveals his characters in four ways:

- through what the characters say to other characters in dialogue
- through what the characters reveal about their thoughts through long speeches to the audience called *soliloquies*
- through what other characters say about them
- through what they do, their actions

As you read the play, examine the following scenes for what they reveal about Brutus' character and fill in the chart briefly using your own words. If you need more room, use the back of the page.

Scene	What Brutus says, does, or what others say about him	What this reveals about Brutus' character
Act II, scene i Brutus contemplates Caesar and meets with Cassius		
Act II, scene ii Brutus comes to accompany Caesar		
Act II, scene iv Portia seeks information about Caesar		

NAME:_____   DATE:_____

During-reading Activity
for
Julius Caesar
Guide to Character Development: Cassius
Act II

Shakespeare reveals his characters in four ways:

ᛞ through what the characters say to other characters in dialogue

ᛞ through what the characters reveal about their thoughts through long speeches to the audience called *soliloquies*

ᛞ through what other characters say about them

ᛞ through what they do, their actions

As you read the play, examine the following scenes for what they reveal about Cassius' character and fill in the chart briefly using your own words. If you need more room, use the back of the page.

Scene	What Cassius says, does, or what others say about him	What this reveals about Cassius' character
Act II, scene i Cassius again meets with Brutus		

NAME:_____   DATE:_____

During-reading Activity
for
Julius Caesar
Guide to Character Development: Antony
Act II

Shakespeare reveals his characters in four ways:

- through what the characters say to other characters in dialogue
- through what the characters reveal about their thoughts through long speeches to the audience called *soliloquies*
- through what other characters say about them
- through what they do, their actions

As you read the play, examine the following scenes for what they reveal about Antony's character and fill in the chart briefly using your own words. If you need more room, use the back of the page.

Scene	What Antony says, does, or what others say about him	What this reveals about Antony's character
Act II, scene i Brutus and others conspire to kill Caesar		
Act II, scene ii Antony comes to accompany Caesar		

During-reading Activity
for
Julius Caesar
Guide to Character Development: Caesar
Act II

Shakespeare reveals his characters in four ways:

- through what the characters say to other characters in dialogue
- through what the characters reveal about their thoughts through long speeches to the audience called *soliloquies*
- through what other characters say about them
- through what they do, their actions

As you read the play, examine the following scenes for what they reveal about Caesar's character and fill in the chart briefly using your own words. If you need more room, use the back of the page.

Scene	*What Caesar says, does, or what others say about him*	*What this reveals about Caesar's character*
Act II, scene i Brutus meets Cassius		
Act II, scene ii Caesar dismisses Calphurnia's dreams		
Act II, scene iii Artemidorus tries to warn Caesar		

During-reading Activity
for
Julius Caesar
Guide to Character Development: Portia
Act II

Shakespeare reveals his characters in four ways:

⁊ through what the characters say to other characters in dialogue

⁊ through what the characters reveal about their thoughts through long speeches to the audience called *soliloquies*

⁊ through what other characters say about them

⁊ through what they do, their actions

As you read the play, examine the following scenes for what they reveal about Portia's character and fill in the chart briefly using your own words. If you need more room, use the back of the page.

Scene	What Portia says, does, or what others say about her	What this reveals about Portia's character
Act II, scene i Portia asks Brutus what's troubling him		
Act II, scene iv Portia sends Lucius to find out about Brutus		

Postreading Activity
for
Julius Caesar
Comprehension Check
Act II

Directions: After you've read all of Act II, use the following questions to check how well you've understood what you've read. For each question, select the most appropriate answer from the choices listed below it. Place the letter corresponding to your answer in the space to the left of the item number.

_____1.   While sitting alone in his garden, Brutus concludes that Caesar

     A. has wronged Brutus and needs to be killed.
     B. has already shown himself to be a tyrant.
     C. is his friend and should be spared.
     D. is harmless at present.
     E. may change his personality when he becomes king.

_____2.   When Cassius suggests that they also kill Antony, Brutus

     A. argues for including Antony in the plot.
     B. argues to let Antony live.
     C. argues to kill only Caesar and his heir, Octavius.
     D. argues to kill Calphurnia instead.
     E. argues to kill both Antony and Caesar secretly.

_____3.   In her dream, Calphurnia has seen

     A. the ghost of her father coming to warn her.
     B. Caesar being stabbed in front of the Capitol.
     C. Caesar being poisoned.
     D. a statue of Caesar spouting blood.
     E. an army overtaking Caesar.

_____4.   To convince Caesar to go to the Senate, Decius

     A. reinterprets Calphurnia's dream.
     B. presents an order from the Senate for Caesar to appear.
     C. threatens to kill Caesar.
     D. threatens to take Calphurnia hostage.
     E. warns him of the plan.

_____5.   Portia asks the Soothsayer about Caesar because

    A. she wants to warn Caesar.
    B. she wants to know about Brutus.
    C. she plans to poison Caesar.
    D. she wants her fortune told.
    E. she has a favor to ask of Caesar.

NAME:_____ DATE:_____

Postreading Activity
for
Julius Caesar
Small Group Discussion to Check Comprehension
Act II

Directions: After you've read all of Act II, in small groups, discuss each of the following questions briefly. Use the space below each question to note points you may want to share later. If you need more room, use the back of the page.

1. In scene i, what has Brutus already concluded about Caesar prior to Cassius' arrival with the other conspirators?

2. In scene i, what reasons does Brutus give for not assassinating Antony along with Caesar?

3. What evidence does Calphurnia offer to support her fears about Caesar's safety?

4. How does Decius convince Caesar to go to the Senate?

5. Why is Portia concerned with Caesar's movements and safety?

Postreading Activity
for
Julius Caesar
Critical Thinking Questions
Act II

Directions: To help develop your understanding of Act II, take time to think about and discuss these questions. The first question should be the focus of your discussion. Don't be concerned that you may not be able to answer it at first. Proceed to the exploration questions and then return to the focus question.

Focus Question. What are the character traits that enable Brutus and other characters in other literature or history that you've read about oppose ignorance and injustice?

Exploration Questions.

1. How would you respond if your school established a policy that everyone with your eye color had to sit in the back of the class, go to lunch last, and stand up at all school functions?

2. In Act II, what does Brutus plan to do in assassinating Caesar that suggests his motives are political rather than personal?

3. From your experience, how do authors use signs, omens, superstitions, or mythology to foreshadow future events in their works?

4. What do you think makes the arguments that eventually convince Brutus to join the conspiracy valid or invalid?

5. In what ways do the signs and omens mentioned in Acts I and II comment upon the action of the play? In what ways do they help foreshadow the assassination of Caesar?

6. How have characters in other works of literature opposed ignorance or injustice?

Postreading Activity
for
Julius Caesar
Language Exploration
Symbol
Act II

When we use a word, object, or image to represent another idea or concept, it becomes a *symbol*. For example, the American flag is a symbol of our country and its democratic form of government.

In literature, too, authors often use symbols. For example, in Act I, scene i, Flavius and Marullus challenge the citizens:

> *What, know you not,*
> *Being mechanical, you ought not walk*
> *Upon a laboring day without the sign*
> *Of your profession?. . . .*
> *Where is thy leather apron, and thy rule?*

Here the types of clothing and equipment a person has identify the worker's trade or profession.

Directions: The following lines from Acts I and II contain symbols. Working in pairs, small groups, or as your teacher directs, review each passage in the context of the play and decide what each symbol suggests to the reader.

   1.   The Soothsayer to Caesar (Act I, scene ii):

> *Beware the ides of March.*

© 1993 by The Center for Applied Research in Education

2. Caesar to Antony, commenting upon Cassius' character (Act I, scene ii):

   Let me have men about me that are fat,
   Sleek—headed men, and such as sleep a-nights.
   Yond Cassius has a lean and hungry look;
   He thinks too much. Such men are dangerous.

3. Casca commenting upon the strange storm to Cicero (Act I, scene iii):

   But never till to-night, never till now,
   Did I go through a tempest dropping fire.
   Either there is civil strife in heaven,
   Or else the world, too saucy with the gods
   Incenses them to send destruction.

4. Cassius commenting to Casca of Caesar's increasing power (Act I, scene iii):

   And why should Caesar be a tyrant then?
   Poor man, I know he would not be a wolf
   But that he sees Romans are but sheep;
   He were no lion, were not the Romans hinds.

85

5. Brutus contemplating how Caesar's personality may change if he becomes king (Act II, scene i):

    &

    It is the bright day that brings forth the adder,
    And that craves wary walking. Crown him that,
    And then I grant we put a sting in him,
    That at his will he may do danger with.

    &

6. Brutus explaining to Cassius why Antony should not be killed too (Act II, scene i):

    &

    Our course will seem too bloody, Caius Cassius,
    To cut the head off, and then hack the limbs,
    Like wrath in death, and envy afterwards;
    Antony is but a limb of Caesar.

    &

7. Calphurnia describing the strange events of the storm to Caesar (Act II, scene ii):

    &

    Fierce fiery warriors fought upon the clouds,
    In ranks and squadrons and right form of war,
    Which drizzled blood upon the Capitol.

    &

8.   Calphurnia relating strange events (Act II, scene ii):

ð

Horses did neigh, and dying men did groan,
And ghosts did shriek and squeal about the streets.

ð

9.   Calphurnia commenting upon the storm (Act II, scene ii):

ð

When beggars die, there are no comets seen;
The heavens themselves blaze forth the death of princes.

ð

10.   Caesar relating Calphurnia's dream to Decius (Act II, scene ii):

ð

She dreamt to-night, she saw my statue,
Which like a fountain with an hundred spouts
Did run pure blood; and many lusty Romans
Came smiling, and did bathe their hands in it.

ð

Postreading Activity
for
Julius Caesar
Vocabulary in Context
Act II

Directions: In each of the passages below you will find one of the words from the prereading vocabulary list for Act II. Review the definitions given in the prereading vocabulary. Working individually, in pairs, or in small groups as your teacher directs, examine each of the underlined words in the following passages from Act II. For each word, use the appropriate meaning and develop a brief interpretation of the passage within the context of the play.

1. Brutus, thinking to himself (scene i):

    It is the bright day that brings forth the adder,
    And that craves <u>wary</u> walking.

2. Brutus, thinking to himself (scene i):

    Fashion it thus; that what he is, augmented,
    Would run to these and these <u>extremities</u>.

3. Brutus to Lucius (scene i):

    🙠

    They are the <u>faction</u>.

    🙠

4. Brutus to Cassius (scene i):

    🙠

    What watchful cares do interpose themselves
    <u>Betwixt</u> your eyes and night?

    🙠

5. Caesar, to himself (scene ii):

    🙠

    <u>Thrice</u> hath Calphurnia in her sleep cried out,
    Help ho, they murder Caesar.

    🙠

6. Caesar to Calphurnia (scene ii):

    🙠

    Cowards die many times before their deaths
    The <u>valiant</u> never taste of death but once.

    🙠

7. Calphurnia to Caesar (scene ii):

ॐ

Let me upon my knee prevail in this.

ॐ

8. Caesar to Decius (scene ii):

ॐ

And these does she apply for warnings and portents
And evils imminent;

ॐ

9. Artemidorus to Caesar (scene iii):

ॐ

If thou read this, o Caesar, thou mayst live;
If not, the Fates with traitors do contrive.

ॐ

10. Portia to Lucius (scene iv):

ॐ

I heard a bustling rumor like a fray
And the wind brings it from the Capitol.

ॐ

© 1993 by The Center for Applied Research in Education

NAME:_____   DATE:_____

Vocabulary Review Quiz
for
Julius Caesar
Act II

Directions: For each of the italicized words in the sentences below, determine which letter best reflects the use of the word in this context. Place the letter corresponding to your answer in the space to the left of the item number.

_____1. Brutus reflects upon the political climate of Rome and knows he must be *wary*.
In this context, *wary* means

A. awake   B. careful   C. lightheaded   D. opportunistic

_____2. Brutus and the others see the assassination of Caesar as a result of the *extremities* of the times.
In this context, *extremities* means

A. time of feeling remote   B. time of waiting   C. time of peace
D. time of extreme need

_____3. Brutus and his followers are a *faction* that supports the restoration of the Roman Republic.
In this context, *faction* means

A. festival   B. political group   C. consensus   D. club

_____4. For Brutus, Caesar stands *betwixt* a dictatorship and the Roman Republic.
In this context, *betwixt* means

A. beneath   B. before   C. beside   D. between

_____5. For Caesar, the *valiant* die only once.
In this context, *valiant* means

A. courageous   B. cowardly   C. thoughtful   D. jealous

_____6. Caesar refused the title of king *thrice*.
In this context, *thrice* means

A. two times   B. five times   C. four times   D. three times

_____7. In the modern world, I still would like to think that justice can *prevail*.
In this context, *prevail* means

A. cease to exist   B. take command   C. win out   D. give up

91

_____ 8. Brutus sees Caesar's quick rise to power as *imminent* to Rome.
In this context, *imminent* means
A. perilous   B. secure   C. prestigious   D. troublesome

_____ 9. The Romans believed that the Fates *contrived* problems in persons'
lives.
In this context, *contrive* means
A. avoided   B. slept   C. played   D. conspired

_____ 10. The argument over the umpire's call soon lead to a *fray*.
In this context, *fray* means
A. unraveling   B. noisy quarrel   C. tantrum   D. tear

ACT III

Focusing Activities
for
Julius Caesar
Scenarios for Improvisation
Act III

Directions: Presented below are locations and situations involving characters. Before reading an individual scene, pretend to be one of the characters and act out the situation. Don't worry about speaking like the characters in Shakespeare's play; just try to imagine how you would react to the situation and use your own language. Take a few minutes to discuss what you would like to do with the other performers. Be prepared to act out your scene for others in the class. Afterward, classmates outside your group can discuss what they've seen.

scene i. *Scene:* The Roman Forum immediately following the assassination of Caesar.

Character: Brutus.

Situation: Improvise how Brutus defends murdering Caesar to the people of Rome.

scene ii. *Scene:* The Roman Forum during Caesar's funeral.

Character: Antony.

Situation: Brutus and the others have allowed Antony to speak at Caesar's funeral, provided Antony does not place blame upon Brutus and the others for Caesar's death. Improvise how Antony turns the crowd against them.

Focusing Activities
for
Julius Caesar
Small Group Discussion Questions
Act III

Directions: Before reading individual scenes in Act III, discuss the questions in small groups. You may wish to make notes about your discussion, so you can share them with classmates or refer back to them after you've read the scene.

scene i.

1. Knowing that Brutus, Cassius, and the others plan to murder Caesar openly, how do you think they will defend their actions to the citizens of Rome?

2. Having seen and heard about Caesar's popularity with the common people, how do you think the people will react when they learn that he has been murdered?

scenes ii.

1. If you were Antony, what would you say at Caesar's funeral that would allow you not only to keep your promise to Brutus and Cassius but also to avenge Caesar's murder?

2. If you were Octavius Caesar, Julius Caesar's nephew and adopted heir, why would it be dangerous for you to return to Rome immediately upon learning of your uncle's death?

scene iii. If you were Shakespeare, how might you show the Romans' reactions to Caesar's death to your audience?

**Focusing Activities
for
Julius Caesar
Speculation Journal
*Act III***

Directions: This activity will help you become involved actively with reading the play by helping you to determine a definite purpose for reading. Before you read these scenes in Act III, take a few minutes to respond in writing to the questions below. Don't worry about correct answers here. Use your own experience or what you have read in the play to speculate about what you think will happen. After reading a scene you may find that the characters reacted differently than you thought. Don't worry about these differences; just make note of them because you will have opportunities to share these differences in other activities.

scene i. If you were one of the conspirators, what advantages would you see in using a public place to attempt to stop Caesar's rise to power? How might you stop him and how would you defend your actions?

scene ii. Based upon what you've seen and heard of the common people's feelings about Caesar, how do you think they will respond to his murder? If you were Brutus, how would you explain your actions to them? If you were one of Caesar's supporters, as Mark Antony is, how might you defend Caesar?

scene iii. Based upon what has happened at Caesar's funeral, how do you expect the common people of Rome to respond to Caesar's assassination?

After Reading Act III: Now that you have finished reading the act, which of your speculations were most accurate? How do you account for them? Which ones were least like the action of the play? Why do you think you speculated as you did?

Prereading Activity
for
Julius Caesar
Vocabulary
Act III

Directions:

scene i

1. **constant** (adj.) certain, unchanging, steadfast, resolute.
   Example: Despite peer pressure, Tricia remained *constant* in her refusal to experiment with drugs.

2. **enterprise** (n.) an important or difficult project.
   Example: NASA's program to get a person on the moon was an extraordinary *enterprise*.

3. **petition** (n.) a respectful or humble request.
   Example: To get permission to use Dad's new car for the prom required a careful *petition* on my part.

4. **redress** (v.) to remedy or correct.
   Example: After stealing the hood ornaments from 150 cars, the boys had to *redress* their mistake by paying to have the cars repaired.

scene ii

5. **censure** (v.) to judge or blame harshly.
   Example: The principal *censured* the students who staged the demonstration by canceling their class trip.

6. **entreat** (v.) to implore or beg.
   Example: Steve *entreated* his parents to buy him the expensive athletic shoes.

7. **extenuate** (v.) to underestimate or underrate; to make a fault seem less serious.
   Example: After the riot, the looters *extenuated* their thievery saying that everyone was doing it.

8. **grievous** (adj.) causing grief; outlandish, atrocious; causing great physical suffering.
   Example: The tornadoes that swept through the town caused many *grievous* injuries.

9. **legacy**   (n.) a gift of property; something of value transferred from one generation to another.

    Example: In my father's family, my great, great grandfather's watch is a *legacy* handed down from father to youngest son.

10. **testament** (n.) a will or formal promise.

    Example: The presidents of the opposing countries signed the treaty and then shook hands as a *testament* to their friendship.

Prereading Activity
for
Julius Caesar
Plot Summaries
Act III

Directions: To help you better understand and follow Shakespeare's play, read the summary of specific scenes immediately before you begin to read the original. If you get lost during the scene, refer to the summary again.

Act III scene i

On the steps of the Capitol, both the Soothsayer and Artemidorus attempt to warn Caesar but fail. Metellus Cimber begs Caesar to repeal the decree that banished his brother. Caesar refuses. The conspirators gather around Caesar and stab him; Brutus is last. Caesar's final words are to his friend Brutus. "And you too, Brutus?"

The assassins declare their reason for killing Caesar: so Rome could remain a Republic rather than become a monarchy. Antony, who has fled, sends his servant to Brutus. Asking not to be harmed, Antony offers to come to Brutus to allow Brutus to explain why Caesar was killed. And if he finds the arguments believable, he promises to support Brutus. Brutus agrees.

When Antony arrives, he says goodbye to Caesar and offers to let the assassins kill him too. Brutus asks Antony to listen to the reasons they give the crowd for killing Caesar. Antony promises and takes the bloody hands of each of the assassins as a token of sharing their actions. Brutus promises to let Antony speak at the funeral, but only if Antony promises not to blame Brutus and the others.

Left alone with Caesar's body, Antony reveals that he shall seek revenge for Caesar's death. When Octavius Caesar's servant tells Antony that Octavius is approaching Rome, Antony warns Octavius not to come until Antony has convinced the crowd to take revenge upon the assassins.

Act III, scene ii

Outside the Capitol in the Forum, Brutus and Cassius appear before the citizens of Rome to speak at Caesar's funeral. Because the people respect Brutus, they allow him to speak. Brutus points out that he was Caesar's friend and admired his bravery. He argues that Caesar was too ambitious and had grown too powerful. The only way to stop Caesar was to kill him in order to preserve the Roman Republic. Brutus introduces Antony who carries in Caesar's body. Brutus seems to have succeeded, for the people accept his arguments, stop calling for his death, and begin to praise him.

© 1993 by The Center for Applied Research in Education

Antony, who has promised not to blame Brutus and the others, then speaks to the people. Throughout the speech, Antony refers to Brutus and the others as honorable men who said Caesar was ambitious. Antony points out that if Caesar were ambitious he's paid for his ambition by dying. To Antony, Caesar was a loyal friend and not an ambitious man. Antony points out that Caesar brought many captives back to Rome who were ransomed and filled the public treasury. Antony states that Caesar was sympathetic to the poor; an ambitious man would have ignored them. As final proof that Caesar wasn't ambitious, Antony reminds the crowd that Caesar refused the crown of king when it was offered to him three times.

The crowd's support for Brutus and the others begins to waiver. They begin to state that Caesar may have been murdered unjustly.

Antony continues. Antony points to the body that no one honors. Antony says that if he were to incite a riot, he would wrong Brutus and Cassius; instead, he would rather wrong Caesar. Antony then pulls out Caesar's will but says this is not the time to read it and tell the people of Rome what Caesar left them. The people beg for Antony to read the will. Antony pretends to be innocent and again suggests that he may have wronged honorable men. The crowd has now turned against Brutus and the others, calling them traitors. They continue to urge Antony to read Caesar's will.

Antony asks to come down from the platform with Caesar's body and have the crowd circle around the corpse. Antony then uncovers the body and attributes specific wounds to individual conspirators. The crowd is horrified and begins to call for revenge. Antony pretends to try to calm them down, knowing that he is inflaming them. Finally Antony reads the will that gives every citizen 75 dracmas. Caesar also leaves the people his orchards and gardens for all to enjoy. The people take Caesar's body to burn in a holy place, which was Roman custom.

The servant of Octavius, Caesar's nephew, then tells Antony that Octavius has arrived.

Act III scene iii   As an example of the people's reaction to Antony's speech, a mob attacks Cinna, the poet. Although the poet has had nothing to do with Caesar's death, the mob carries him off and kills him because he has the same name as one of the conspirators.

Class Period:

CHARACTER ASSIGNMENTS FOR ORAL READING GROUPS

Julius Caesar

Session 3: Act III

Characters	*Group 1*	*Group 2*	*Group 3*	*Group 4*
Antony, Caesar, Cinna, the poet				
Soothsayer, Metellus, First Citizen				
Decius, Second Citizen				
Artemidorus, Third Citizen, Trebonius				
Popilius, Servant, Fourth Citizen				
Cassius				
Brutus				
Cinna, Publius				

104

During-reading Activity
for
Julius Caesar
Character Diary 3
Act III, scenes i, ii, iii

Directions: Use the space below to record your character's reactions to the events of Act III in *Julius Caesar*. Remember to include a summary of events, explain how your character learned of them, and give your character's reactions to these events. Because the act contains three scenes, you may want to record your character's entries as you read each scene. If you need additional room, use the back of this sheet.

The Personal Diary of

_____
(character's name)

Rome
March 15, 44 B.C.
Evening

_____
_____
_____
_____
_____
_____
_____
_____
_____
_____
_____
_____
_____

NAME:_____   DATE:_____

During-reading Activities
for
Julius Caesar
Viewing Act III, scenes i and ii
Caesar's Assassination and Funeral

Directions: Read this scene before viewing a video of it. Viewing the film or video version should help you to better understand how the text translates into the characters' motives and actions. Although you may want to keep your copy of the play handy, don't be surprised if the actors' script varies from your own. Film scripts often delete or reorder the lines of the play. You may want to note questions to ask after you have seen the video. After viewing the scene, take a few minutes to respond to the questions below.

1. Based upon what you've seen, what aspects of Caesar's character make it possible for the assassins to get close enough to kill him?

2. What additional information does seeing the video provide you that helps you understand the characters and their motivations?

3. How just does Brutus' defense for killing Caesar sound? How just does Antony's funeral oration sound? How do the actors' facial expressions, tones of voice, and gestures enhance Shakespeare's words?

During-reading Activity
for
Julius Caesar
Guide to Character Development: Brutus
Act III

Shakespeare reveals his characters in four ways:

- ◆ through what the characters say to other characters in dialogue
- ◆ through what the characters reveal about their thoughts through long speeches to the audience called *soliloquies*
- ◆ through what other characters say about them
- ◆ through what they do, their actions

As you read the play, examine the following scenes for what they reveal about Brutus' character and fill in the chart briefly using your own words. If you need more room, use the back of the page.

Scene	*What Brutus says, does, or what others say about him*	*What this reveals about Brutus' character*
Act III, scene i Brutus helps to assassinate Caesar		
Act III, scene ii Brutus speaks at Caesar's funeral		
Act III, scene iii Mob kills Cinna, the poet		

**During-reading Activity
for
Julius Caesar
*Guide to Character Development: Cassius
Act III***

Shakespeare reveals his characters in four ways:

- through what the characters say to other characters in dialogue
- through what the characters reveal about their thoughts through long speeches to the audience called *soliloquies*
- through what other characters say about them
- through what they do, their actions

As you read the play, examine the following scenes for what they reveal about Cassius' character and fill in the chart briefly using your own words. If you need more room, use the back of the page.

Scene	What Cassius says, does, or what others say about him	What this reveals about Cassius' character
Act III, scene i Cassius helps to assassinate Caesar		
Act III, scene ii Antony delivers funeral oration		
Act III, scene iii Mob kills Cinna, the poet		

NAME:_____   DATE:_____

During-reading Activity
for
Julius Caesar
Guide to Character Development: Antony
Act III

Shakespeare reveals his characters in four ways:

- ❧ through what the characters say to other characters in dialogue
- ❧ through what the characters reveal about their thoughts through long speeches to the audience called *soliloquies*
- ❧ through what other characters say about them
- ❧ through what they do, their actions

As you read the play, examine the following scenes for what they reveal about Antony's character and fill in the chart briefly using your own words. If you need more room, use the back of the page.

Scene	What Antony says, does, or what others say about him	What this reveals about Antony's character
Act III, scene i Caesar is killed		
Act III, scene ii Antony delivers funeral oration		
Act III, scene iii Mob kills Cinna, the poet		

© 1993 by The Center for Applied Research in Education

NAME:_____   DATE:_____

During-reading Activity
for
Julius Caesar
Guide to Character Development: Caesar
Act III

Shakespeare reveals his characters in four ways:

- through what the characters say to other characters in dialogue
- through what the characters reveal about their thoughts through long speeches to the audience called *soliloquies*
- through what other characters say about them
- through what they do, their actions

As you read the play, examine the following scenes for what they reveal about Caesar's character and fill in the chart briefly using your own words. If you need more room, use the back of the page.

Scene	What Caesar says, does, or what others say about him	What this reveals about Caesar's character
Act III, scene i Caesar is killed		
Act III, scene ii Antony eulogizes Caesar		
Act III, scene iii Mob kills Cinna, the poet		

© 1993 by The Center for Applied Research in Education

Postreading Activity
for
Julius Caesar
Comprehensive Check
Act III

Directions: After you've read all of Act III, use the following questions to check how well you've understood what you've read. For each question, select the most appropriate answer from the choices listed below it. Place the letter corresponding to your answer in the space to the left of the item number.

_____1.   Immediately after the conspirators stab Caesar,

A. Antony proclaims himself king.
B. Cassius orders the arrest of Calphurnia.
C. Antony flees.
D. Octavius takes his uncle's place.
E. Brutus commits suicide.

_____2.   Brutus agrees to let Antony speak at Caesar's funeral but

A. Brutus must speak after Antony.
B. Antony can only place blame on Caesar.
C. Brutus gets to ignite the funeral pyre.
D. Brutus gets to blame Antony for Caesar's death.
E. Antony may not blame any of the conspirators.

_____3.   At Caesar's funeral, Brutus

A. explains that he killed Caesar for the good of Rome.
B. explains the he killed Caesar in self-defense.
C. explains Caesar's death as an accident.
D. begs forgiveness from the crowd.
E. incites the citizens to continue the rebellion against Antony and Octavius.

111

_____ 4. During his funeral oration, Antony

A. points out Caesar's good points.
B. refers to Brutus as honorable.
C. goes back on his promise to Brutus.
D. promises to reward anyone who will kill Brutus.
E. kills himself.

_____ 5. Whom does the mob apparently kill in scene iii?

A. Brutus
B. Cassius
C. Cinna, the poet
D. Cinna, the senator
E. Casca

Postreading Activity
for
Julius Caesar
Small Group Discussion to Check Comprehension
Act III

Directions: After you've read all of Act III, in small groups, discuss each of the following questions briefly. Use the space below each question to note points you may wish to share later. If you need more room, use the back of the page.

1. How does Brutus justify the assassination of Julius Caesar to the citizens of Rome?

2. What conditions does Brutus impose on what Antony may say at Caesar's funeral?

3. How does Antony go about turning the people of Rome against Brutus, Cassius, and the other conspirators?

4. What does the death of Cinna, the poet, show the audience about the reaction of the people of Rome to Caesar's death?

NAME:_____   DATE:_____

Postreading Activity
for
Julius Caesar
Critical Thinking Questions
Act III

Directions: To help you develop your understanding of Act II, take time to think about and discuss these questions. The first question should be the focus of your discussion. Don't be concerned that you may not be able to answer it at first. Proceed to the exploration questions and then return to the focus question.

Focus Question. In what situation would you feel justified in manipulating a situation with language or by other means as Antony does in his funeral oration?

Exploration Questions.

1.   Relate an experience you've had where you used either a literal interpretation of language to take advantage of someone else or someone used language to take advantage of you. To help you recall such a situation, start with one in which you or the other person provided a defense of the action with "But you never said I couldn't. . . ."

2.   In works of literature that you've read, how have characters used the interpretation of language to their own advantage in a situation?

3.   How well do you feel Antony honors the conditions Brutus imposes upon him about speaking at Caesar's funeral?

4.   In what ways does your own experience (*see* question 1 above) compare with the situations of characters in other literature that have used language to their own advantage?

5.   Compare your experience (from question 1) with Antony's use of language in the funeral oration (Act III, scene ii).

6.   How does Antony's use of language in the funeral oration compare with that of characters in literature that you've read?

Postreading Activity
for
Julius Caesar
Language Exploration
Verbal Irony
Act III

Imagine that while you're in the school cafeteria, someone drops his/her tray. One of your friends begins applauding and yells out "Way to go, Grace!" More than likely, you'll probably begin to laugh because there's a discrepancy between what your friend said and what occurred. Dropping the tray is not a sign of graceful coordination. When we say one thing and mean another, it is an example of *verbal irony*. Verbal irony is often used in literature. Either the author or a character may say one thing and mean another. This is often the case in Shakespeare's plays.

Directions: The following passages contain examples of verbal irony. Working in pairs, small groups, or as your teacher directs, review each passage in the context of the play and decide how what the character says differs from what the character means.

1.   Cassius speaking to Brutus about Caesar (Act I, scene ii):

&

> *Why man, he doth bestride the narrow world*
> *Like a Colossus, and we petty men*
> *Walk under his huge legs and peep about*
> *To find ourselves dishonorable graves.*

&

2.   Once Brutus has agreed to think over what Cassius has said, Cassius responds (Act I, scene ii):

&

> *I am glad*
> *That my weak words have struck but this much show*
> *Of fire from Brutus.*

&

3. When Brutus and Cassius ask Casca to describe how Caesar refused the crown, Casca remarks (Act I, scene ii):

I can as well be hanged as tell the manner of it. It was mere foolery; I did not mark it.

4. Casca responds to the effect of Cicero's speaking in Greek to the crowd (Act I, scene ii):

Nay, an I tell you that, I'll never look you i' th' face again. But those that understood him smiled at one another, and shook their heads; but mine own part, it was Greek to me.

5. When Casca meets Cassius during the storm (Act I, scene iii) he asks "what night it is." Cassius replies:

A very pleasing night to honest men.

6. Cassius' response to learning that the Senate plans to make Caesar king (Act I, scene iii):

&

O know where I will wear this dagger then;
Cassius from bondage will deliver Cassius.

&

7. After Decius reinterprets Calphurnia's dream (Act II, scene ii), Caesar replies to his wife:

&

How foolish do your fears seem now Calphurnia!

&

8. When the conspirators come to escort Caesar, he welcomes them (Act II, scene ii):

&

Welcome Publius.
What Brutus, are you stirred so early too?
Good morrow Casca. Caius Ligarius,
Caesar was ne'er so much your enemy
As that same ague that has made you lean.

&

9. When Cassius questions the wisdom of allowing Antony to speak at Caesar's funeral (Act III, scene i), Brutus replies:

❧

What Antony shall speak, I will protest
He speaks by leave, and by permission;
And that we are contented Caesar shall
Have all true rites, and lawful ceremonies.
It shall advantage more than do wrong.

❧

10. During the funeral oration (Act III, scene ii), Antony states repeatedly:

❧

. . .Brutus is an honorable man.

❧

NAME:_____   DATE:_____

Postreading Activity
for
Julius Caesar
Vocabulary in Context
Act III

Directions: In each of the passages below you will find one of the words from the prereading vocabulary list for Act III. Review the definitions, working individually, in pairs, or in small groups as your teacher directs, examining each of the underlined words. For each word, use the appropriate meaning and develop a brief interpretation of the passage within the context of the play.

1. Cassius to Artemidorus and Publius (scene i):

   ❧

   What, urge you your <u>petitions</u> in the street?
   Come to the Capitol.

   ❧

2. Popilius to Cassius (scene i):

   ❧

   I wish your <u>enterprise</u> today may thrive.

   ❧

3. Caesar to Cinna (scene i):

   ❧

   What is now amiss,
   That Caesar and his senate must <u>redress</u>.

   ❧

© 1993 by The Center for Applied Research in Education

119

4.   Caesar to Publius Cimber (scene i):

ɞ

But I am <u>constant</u> as the northern star,
Of whose true-fixed and resting quality
There is no fellow in the firmament.

ɞ

5.   Brutus to the crowd (scene ii):

ɞ

Believe me for mine honor, and have respect to mine honor,
that you may believe. <u>Censure</u> me in your wisdom,
and awake your senses, that you may be the better judge.

ɞ

6.   Brutus to the crowd (scene ii):

ɞ

I have done no more to Caesar than you shall do to Brutus.
The question of his death is enrolled in the Capitol;
his glory is not <u>extenuated</u>, wherein he was worthy;
nor his offenses enforced for which he suffered death.

ɞ

7.   Brutus to the crowd (scene ii):

❧

I do <u>entreat</u> you, not a man depart,
Save I alone, till Antony have spoke.

❧

8.   Antony to the crowd (scene ii):

❧

The noble Brutus
Hath told you Caesar was ambitious;
If it were so, it was a <u>grievous</u> fault,
And <u>grievously</u> hath Caesar answered it.

❧

9.   Antony to crowd (scene ii):

❧

I found it in his closet, 'tis his will
Let but the commons hear this <u>testament</u>—

❧

10.   Antony to crowd (scene ii):

❧

Yea, beg a hair of him for memory,
And dying, mention it in their wills,
Bequeathing it as a rich <u>legacy</u>
Unto their issue.

❧

Vocabulary Review Quiz
for
Julius Caesar
Act III

Directions: For each of the italicized words in the sentences below, determine which letter best reflects the use of the word in this context. Place the letter corresponding to your answer in the space to the left of the item number.

_____1. Once Brutus agrees to the assassination of Caesar, he is *constant* in his loyalty to Cassius.
In this context, *constant* means

A. steadfast   B. changeable   C. absent   D. unknown quantity

_____2. Columbus' first expedition was not a profitable *enterprise*.
In this context *enterprise* means

A. celebration   B. event   C. difficult project   D. adventure

_____3. Artemidorus presents his *petition* to Caesar in the street.
In this context, *petition* means

A. letter   B. unreasonable demand   C. respectful request
D. reasonable demand

_____4. Just prior to Caesar's assassination, Caesar offers to *redress* anyone's wrongs.
In this context, *redress* means

A. correct   B. search   C. punish   D. avenge

_____5. At Caesar's funeral, Brutus urges the crowd to think critically before they *censure* his actions.
In this context, *censure* means

A. correct   B. commend   C. judge harshly   D. disclose

_____6. Brutus also *entreats* the crowd to stay until after Antony has spoken.
In this context, *entreat* means

A. bribes   B. begs   C. shames   D. orders

_____7. When Brutus speaks to the crowd at Caesar's funeral, he does not *extenuate* Caesar's accomplishments.
In this context, *extenuate* means

A. underrate   B. overrate   C. deny   D. state

© 1993 by The Center for Applied Research in Education

_____8. Brutus feels that Caesar's most *grievous* fault was his ambition.
In this context, *grievous* means

A. changing   B. troublesome   C. joyous   D. causing

_____9. Caesar's *legacy* to the citizens of Rome was his private gardens.
In this context, *legacy* means

A. inheritance   B. monument   C. gift   D. tax

_____10. As a *testament* to his devotion, the millionaire left $500,000 to the college.
In this context, *testament* means

A. statement   B. courtesy   C. formal promise   D. book

ACT IV

NAME:_____   DATE:_____

Focusing Activities
for
Julius Caesar
Scenarios for Improvisation
Act IV

Directions: Presented below are locations and situations involving characters. Before reading an individual scene, pretend to be one of the characters and act out the situation. Don't worry about speaking like the characters in Shakespeare's play; just try to imagine how you would react to the situation and use your own language. Take a few minutes to discuss with the other performers what you would like to do. Be prepared to act out your scene for others in the class. Afterward, classmates outside your group can discuss what they've seen.

scene i.   *Scene:* Antony's house.

Characters: Octavius and Antony.

Situation: Antony and Octavius plot revenge upon Brutus, Cassius, and the other conspirators for the murder of Caesar. Improvise the dialogue between them.

scene ii.   *Scene:* Brutus' camp.

Characters: Brutus and Cassius.

Situation: Brutus has had one of Cassius' generals killed for taking bribes. Cassius, who had defended the general in a letter to Brutus, is angry because his defense was ignored. Although both men know that their survival depends upon their remaining allies, Cassius confronts Brutus about the situation. Improvise the dialogue between them.

NAME:_____   DATE:_____

Focusing Activities
for
Julius Caesar
Small Group Discussion Questions
Act IV

Directions: Before reading scenes in Act IV, discuss the questions in small groups. You may wish to make notes about your discussion, so you can share them with classmates or refer back to them after you've read the scene.

scene i. If you were Octavius and Antony, what plans would you make to avenge the murder of Julius Caesar and to seize his power?

scenes ii and iii.

1. How might the differences in the reasons Brutus and Cassius had for murdering Caesar create problems for their remaining allies against Antony and Octavius?

2. Besides being part of the conspiracy to murder Caesar, what other bonds of friendship do Cassius and Brutus have?

NAME:_____   DATE:_____

Focusing Activities
for
Julius Caesar
Speculation Journal
Act IV

Directions: This activity will help you become involved actively with reading the play by helping you to determine a definite purpose for reading. Before you read these scenes in Act IV, take a few minutes to respond in writing to the questions below. Don't worry about correct answers here. Use your own experience or what you have read in the play to speculate about what you think will happen. After reading a scene you may find that the characters reacted differently than you thought. Don't worry about these differences; just make note of them because you will have opportunities to share these differences in other activities.

scene i.   What do you think Mark Antony and Octavius Caesar, as supporters of Julius Caesar, will do to avenge the murder of Julius Caesar?

scenes ii and iii.   How do you think Brutus and Cassius will respond to Antony, Octavius, and Lepidus seeking out and killing the other conspirators systematically? At this point in the play, why do you feel it is necessary for Brutus and Cassius to remain united?

After Reading Act IV: Now that you have finished reading Act IV, which of your speculations were most accurate? How do you account for them? Which ones were least like the action of the play? Why do you think you speculated as you did?

129

Prereading Activity
for
Julius Caesar
Vocabulary
Act IV

Directions: Shakespeare uses the following words in Act IV. The section below provides a brief definition of each word and provides a sentence to illustrate its meaning.

Definitions

scene i

1. **prick**   (n.) a mark made by pricking; a dot, a point.
   (v.) to mark by pricking, urge forward.
   Example: Octavius and Antony placed dots or *pricks* beside the names of traitors.

2. **provender** (n.) dry food for livestock.
   Example: Hay and grain are common types of *provender*.

3. **levy**   (n.) raising or collecting an army or money by authority or force.
   (v.) to collect or impose a tax.
   Example: In feudal England, a lord had the power to *levy* taxes to raise and support his army.

scene ii

4. **instance**   (n.) a presence, a cause, a mark.
   Example: The principal's *instance* in the classroom reduced the noise level considerably.

5. **mettle**   (n.) characteristic disposition or temperament.
   Example: Although Bruce failed to break any records during practice, he demonstrated his *mettle* by setting a new school record during the race.

scene iii

6. **chastise-ment:**   (n.) the act of disciplining or restraining behavior; punishment.
   Example: The school board instituted in-school suspension as a *chastisement* for unruly students.

7. **fret**   (v.) to feel or express annoyance, concern, or worry.
   Example: Barry *fretted* until he learned that he had passed his algebra exam.

8. **slight**   (v.) to treat with little importance.
   Example: As vacation approaches, students may *slight* their school work.

9. **testy**   (adj.) irritably impatient; touchy.
   Example: After Mike's parents grounded him for a week, he was *testy* the rest of the day.

10. **vex**   (v.) to irritate, annoy, or provoke.
    Example: It's not uncommon for younger brothers to vex their older sisters.

131

Prereading Activity
for
Julius Caesar
Plot Summaries
Act IV

Directions: To help you better understand and follow Shakespeare's play, read the summary of specific scenes immediately before you begin to read the original. If you get lost during the scene, refer to the summary again.

Act IV,
scene i

At home, Antony meets with Octavius and Lepidus. They agree to seek revenge upon all the conspirators even though two of them are members of their own families (Lepidus' brother and Antony's nephew). Antony sends Lepidus to fetch Caesar's will.

Antony confides to Octavius that he doesn't really want to share power with Lepidus. Octavius points out that Lepidus is a good soldier and that they need him for now, because Brutus and Cassius are gaining power and raising an army.

Act IV,
scene ii

Many months later, Brutus and Cassius have camped their armies near Sardis. Cassius sends his servant Pindarus to greet Brutus. Brutus feels that Cassius has mishandled some things but will accept Cassius' explanation. Brutus pulls Lucilius aside and asks how Cassius treated Lucilius when Brutus sent a message. Lucilius notes that Cassius was courteous but not as friendly as he normally is.

When Cassius arrives, he's angry with Brutus and demands an explanation. Brutus urges Cassius to discuss his grievance inside rather than in front of their armies.

Act IV,
scene iii

Once inside Brutus' tent, Cassius is angry with Brutus for condemning Lucius Pella for taking bribes from the Sardians after Cassius defended Pella in a letter. Brutus' reply is that Cassius was wrong to defend Pella and that Cassius has also been known to take bribes. Brutus reminds Cassius that they killed Caesar to insure justice, so they must be more careful in their own lives not to give anyone evidence that they are corrupt. Cassius is angry and begins to threaten Brutus. Brutus sarcastically urges him to get angry and out of control and then go show his army what kind of a madman leads them. Brutus knows that Cassius' words are empty threats. Brutus then accuses Cassius of denying him the money he requested to pay his troops. Brutus would rather get the money from his friend than make it dis-

© 1993 by The Center for Applied Research in Education

honestly by preying upon the local peasants. Cassius' reply is that the messenger got the message wrong.

Cassius then tells Brutus that friends should overlook each others' faults. Brutus points out that a flatterer would overlook the faults but not a friend. They both realize that they were speaking in anger and resolve their quarrel.

Brutus then tells Cassius that Portia, fearing the power of Antony and Octavius, swallowed fire and killed herself. They then drink to their friendship.

Tintinius and Messala bring news that Octavius, Antony, and Lepidus have seized power and put a hundred senators to death. Their armies now approach Philippi. Brutus suggests he and Cassius move their armies to Philippi. Cassius would rather remain in Sardis and make the other army come to them, so Brutus' and Cassius' armies will be rested and better able to fight. But Brutus points out that the people between Sardis and Philippi have only supported them grudgingly. Antony and Octavius' forces would probably gain support from these people, so Cassius agrees to march to Philippi.

Once Cassius is gone, Brutus prepares to go to bed. Brutus asks Varro and Claudius to stay in his tent. To quiet the troubled Brutus, Lucius sings a song. It relaxes Brutus and lulls Varro and Claudius to sleep. The ghost of Julius Caesar then appears with a warning: " I'll see you again at Philippi." Brutus arouses the others, but no one else saw the ghost. Brutus then sends Varro and Claudius to tell Cassius to begin the march to Philippi.

Class Period:

CHARACTER ASSIGNMENTS FOR ORAL READING GROUPS

Julius Caesar

Session 4: Act IV

Characters	*Group 1*	*Group 2*	*Group 3*	*Group 4*
Antony, Pindarus, Claudius	_____	_____	_____	_____
Lepidus, First Soldier, Varro	_____	_____	_____	_____
Octavius, Third Soldier, Tintinius, Lucius	_____	_____	_____	_____
Brutus	_____	_____	_____	_____
Cassius	_____	_____	_____	_____
Lucilius, poet	_____	_____	_____	_____
Second Soldier, Messala, Ghost of Caesar	_____	_____	_____	_____

134

NAME:_____   **DATE:**_____

During-reading Activity
for
Julius Caesar
Character Diary 4
Act IV, scenes i, ii, and iii

Directions: Use the space below to record your character's reactions to the events of Act IV in *Julius Caesar*. Remember to include a summary of events, explain how your character learned of them, and give your character's reactions to these events. Because the act contains three scenes, you may wish to record your character's entries as you read each scene. If you need additional room, use the back of this sheet.

The Personal Diary of

_____
(character's name)

Act IV, scene i.
Rome·

_____, 44 B.C. (A few days or months after the assassination.)

_____

_____

_____

_____

Act IV, scenes ii and iii.
Sardis

_____, 43 B.C. (Many months later.)

_____

_____

_____

_____

_____

135

NAME:_____   DATE:_____

During-reading Activity
for
Julius Caesar
Viewing Act IV, scenes ii and iii
Brutus and Cassius' Quarrel

Directions: Read this scene before viewing a video of it. Viewing the film or video version should help you better understand how the text translates into the characters' motives and actions. Although you may want to keep your copy of the play handy, don't be surprised if the actors' script varies from your own. Film scripts often delete or reorder the lines of the play. You may want to note questions to ask after you have seen the video. After viewing the scene, take a few minutes to respond to the questions below.

1. Based upon what you've seen, why do Brutus and Cassius need to move inside Brutus' tent to continue their discussion?

2. Brutus and Cassius' quarrel is still the central issue in this scene. How do the actors' facial expressions, tones of voice, and gestures help you understand each character's position?

NAME:_____   DATE:_____

During-reading Activity
for
Julius Caesar
Guide to Character Development: Brutus
Act IV

Shakespeare reveals his characters in four ways:

- through what the characters say to other characters in dialogue
- through what the characters reveal about their thoughts through long speeches to the audience called *soliloquies*
- through what other characters say about them
- through what they do, their actions

As you read the play, examine the following scenes for what they reveal about Brutus' character and fill in the chart briefly using your own words. If you need more room, use the back of the page.

Scene	*What Brutus says, does, or what others say about him*	*What this reveals about Brutus' character*
Act IV, scene i Antony, Lepidus, and Octavius plot revenge against conspirators		
Act IV, scenes ii, iii Brutus and Cassius meet at Sardis		

NAME:_____   DATE:_____

During-reading Activity
for
Julius Caesar
Guide to Character Development: Cassius
Act IV

Shakespeare reveals his characters in four ways:

- 🙤 through what the characters say to other characters in dialogue

- 🙤 through what the characters reveal about their thoughts through long speeches to the audience called *soliloquies*

- 🙤 through what other characters say about them

- 🙤 through what they do, their actions

As you read the play, examine the following scenes for what they reveal about Cassius' character and fill in the chart briefly using your own words. If you need more room, use the back of the page.

Scene	What Cassius says, does, or what others say about him	What this reveals about Cassius' character
Act IV, scene i Antony, Lepidus, and Octavius plot revenge against conspirators		
Act IV, scenes ii, iii Cassius and Brutus meet at Sardis		

© 1993 by The Center for Applied Research in Education

During-reading Activity
for
Julius Caesar
Guide to Character Development: Antony
Act IV

Shakespeare reveals his characters in four ways:

- through what the characters say to other characters in dialogue
- through what the characters reveal about their thoughts through long speeches to the audience called *soliloquies*
- through what other characters say about them
- through what they do, their actions

As you read the play, examine the following scenes for what they reveal about Antony's character and fill in the chart briefly using your own words. If you need more room, use the back of the page.

Scene	*What Antony says, does, or what others say about him*	*What this reveals about Antony's character*
Act IV, scene i Antony and Octavius plot revenge against conspirators		

NAME:_____ DATE: _____

During-reading Activity
for
Julius Caesar
Guide to Character Development: Portia
Act IV

Shakespeare reveals his characters in four ways:

- through what the characters say to other characters in dialogue
- through what the characters reveal about their thoughts through long speeches to the audience called *soliloquies*
- through what other characters say about them
- through what they do, their actions

As you read the play, examine the following scenes for what they reveal about Portia's character and fill in the chart briefly using your own words. If you need more room, use the back of the page.

Scene	What Portia says, does, or what others say about her	What this reveals about Portia's character
Act IV, scene iii Cassius tells Brutus of Portia's suicide		

NAME:_____   DATE:_____

Postreading Activity
for
Julius Caesar
Comprehension Check
Act IV

Directions: After you've read all of Act IV, use the following questions to check how well you've understood what you've read. For each question, select the most appropriate answer from the choices listed below it. Place the letter corresponding to your answer in the space to the left of the item number.

_____ 1. As they plan to avenge Caesar's death in scene i, Antony and Octavius agree to

A. kill members of their own families.
B. kill all the Senators in Rome.
C. kill Brutus' and Cassius' families.
D. kill Brutus and Cassius.
E. kill themselves.

_____ 2. Antony and Octavius consent to include Lepidus in their plans because

A. he is a brilliant military strategist.
B. he serves their purposes for the time being.
C. he is clever and will only follow orders.
D. he is wealthy.
E. he is Brutus and Cassius' best friend.

_____ 3. Cassius is angry with Brutus because

A. Lucius Pella stole from him.
B. Brutus took a bribe from Lucius Pella.
C. Brutus ignored Cassius' defense of Pella.
D. Brutus killed Pella without a trial.
E. Brutus tried to bribe Pella.

_____ 4. Brutus defends his condemning of Lucius Pella because

A. Pella was corrupt.
B. to condone bribery would make their plot to kill Caesar look corrupt.
C. it was a just action.
D. there wasn't time to consult Cassius.
E. their army needed money.

141

_____5.   In the following lines, what reason does Brutus give for the march to Philippi?

The people 'twixt Philippi and this ground
Do stand but in a forced affection;
For they have grudged us contribution.
The enemy, marching along by them
By them shall make a fuller number up,
Come on refreshed, new-added, and encouraged;
From which advantage shall we cut him off,
If at Philippi we do face him there,
These people at our back.

A. The Philippians are stronger soldiers and can stand the march.
B. He wishes to take Antony and Octavius by surprise.
C. He has already agreed to meet Antony and Octavius there.
D. Antony and Octavius' army is tired.
E. The Philippians would join Antony and Octavius' forces if they stay.

Postreading Activity
for
Julius Caesar
Small Group Discussion to Check Comprehension
Act IV

Directions: After you've read all of Act IV, in small groups, or as your teacher directs, discuss each of the following questions briefly. Use the space below each question to note points you may want to share later.

1. What are Antony and Octavius willing to do to avenge Caesar's death?

2. What is Cassius' position in his quarrel with Brutus?

3. What is Brutus' position in the quarrel with Cassius?

4. What does the means by which Portia committed suicide say about her character?

NAME:_____   DATE:_____

Postreading Activity
for
Julius Caesar
Critical Thinking Questions
Act IV

Directions: To help develop your understanding of Act IV, take time to think about and discuss these questions. The first question is the focus question and the point of the discussion. Don't be concerned that you may not be able to answer it at first. Proceed to the exploration questions and then return to the focus question.

Focus Question. Is revenge honorable even if it means sacrificing your family as Antony and Octavius do?

Exploration Questions.

1. What must someone do to you in order to make you seek revenge?

2. Why does Brutus condemn Lucius Pella, one of Cassius' generals, for taking bribes?

3. In other plays, poems, stories, or novels that you have read, how has a character sought revenge upon another?

4. Do you feel Brutus is justified in punishing Lucius Pella for taking bribes even though he knows this action may jeopardize his alliance with Cassius?

5. How do you think Brutus' motives for both assassinating Caesar and for punishing Lucius Pella would be received today?

6. Do you think seeking revenge is either noble or honorable in modern society?

© 1993 by The Center for Applied Research in Education

144

NAME: _____   DATE: _____

Postreading Activity
for
Julius Caesar
Language Exploration
Imagery
Act IV

In addition to figurative language, symbolism, and verbal irony, Shakespeare also uses *imagery:* language that appeals to the senses of sight, touch, taste, smell, and hearing. Because our senses provide our direct contact with the world, poets often appeal to these concrete experiences to help convey more abstract ideas. Shakespeare often develops imagery in combination with figurative language.

Notice how Cassius appeals to the senses to emphasize his point that both Brutus and Caesar are noble men (Act I, scene ii):

ぼ

Brutus and Caesar. What should be in that Caesar?
Why should that name be sounded more than yours? (sound—hearing)
Write them together, yours is as fair a name. (sight)
Sound them, it doth become the mouth as well. (sound—speech)
Weigh them, it is as heavy. (touch)

ぼ

Directions: The following passages from Acts III and IV contain examples of imagery. Working in pairs, small groups, or as your teacher directs, review each passage in the context of the play and decide which sense Shakespeare appeals to and what the passage suggests to the reader.

1. Caesar refusing Publius Cimber's request to permit his brother to return from exile (Act III, scene i):

ぼ

But I am constant as the northern star,
Of whose true-fixed and resting quality
There is no fellow in the firmament.
The skies are painted with unnumbered sparks,
They are all fire and every one doth shine;
But there's but one in all doth hold his place.

ぼ

145

2. Antony addressing Caesar's bleeding corpse (Act III, scene i):

    Had I as many eyes as thou hast wounds,
    Weeping as fast as they stream forth thy blood,
    It would become me better than to close
    In terms of friendship with thine enemies.

3. Antony promising revenge for Caesar's murder (Act III, scene i):

    Over thy wounds now I do prophesy,
    Which like dumb mouths do ope their ruby lips
    To beg the voice and utterance of my tongue.
    A curse shall light upon the limbs of men;

4. Antony calling for vengeance (Act III, scene ii):

    Cry havoc, and let slip the dogs of war,
    That this foul deed shall smell above the earth
    With carrion men, groaning for burial.

5.   Antony to Octavius describing Lepidus (Act IV, scene i):

&

To ease ourselves of divers sland'rous loads,
He shall but bear them as an ass bears gold,
To groan and sweat under the business,
Either led or driven, as we point the way;
And having brought our treasure where we will,
Then take we down his load, and turn him off,
And graze in commons.

&

6.   Brutus commenting on Cassius' less friendly welcome of Pindarus (Act IV, scene ii):

&

Thou hast described
A hot friend cooling.

&

7.   Brutus pointing out to Cassius his history of taking bribes (Act IV, scene iii):

&

Let me tell you Cassius, you yourself
Are much condemned to have an itching palm,
To sell and mart your offices for gold
To undeservers.

&

147

8. Brutus to Cassius (Act IV, scene iii):

    ❧

    I had rather be a dog, and bay the moon.

    ❧

9. Brutus to Cassius (Act IV, scene iii):

    ❧

    There is no terror in your threats;
    For I am armed so strong in honesty,
    That they pass by me, as the idle wind.

    ❧

10. Brutus commenting on the strength of his forces (Act IV, scene iii):

    ❧

    There is a tide in the affairs of men,
    Which taken at the flood leads on to fortune;
    Omitted, all the voyage of their life
    Is bound in shallows and in miseries.
    On such a full sea are we now afloat
    And we must take the current when it serves,
    Or lose our ventures.

    ❧

Postreading Activity
for
Julius Caesar
Vocabulary in Context
Act IV

Directions: In each of the passages below you will find one of the words from the prereading vocabulary list for Act IV. Review the definitions given in the prereading vocabulary. Working individually, in pairs, or in small groups as your teacher directs, examine each of the underlined words in the following passages from Act IV. For each word, use the appropriate meaning and develop a brief interpretation of the passage within the context of the play.

1.   Octavius to Antony and Lepidus (scene i):

಺

> *So you thought him,*
> *And took his voice who should be <u>pricked</u> to die,*
> *In our black sentence and proscription.*

಺

2.   Antony to Octavius and Lepidus (scene i)

಺

> *So is my horse Octavius, and for that*
> *I do appoint him store of <u>provender</u>,*

಺

3.   Antony to Octavius and Lepidus (scene i):

🙂

Brutus and Cassius
Are <u>levying</u> powers; we must straight make head.

🙂

4.   Lucilius to Brutus (scene ii):

🙂

With courtesy, and with respect enough,
But not with such familiar <u>instances</u>,
Nor with such free and friendly conference
As he hath used of old.

🙂

5.   Brutus reflecting upon men's characters (scene ii):

🙂

But hollow men, like horses hot at hand,
Make gallant show, and promise of their <u>mettle</u>;

🙂

6. Cassius defending Lucius Pella to Brutus (scene iii):

    &

    Wherein my letters, praying on his side,
    Because I knew the man, was <u>slighted</u> off.

    &

7. Brutus to Cassius (scene iii):

    &

    The name of Cassius honors this corruption,
    And <u>chastisement</u> doth therefore hide his head.

    &

8. Brutus to Cassius (scene iii):

    &

    All this? Ay more. <u>Fret</u> till your proud heart break.

    &

9.   Brutus to Cassius (scene iii):

❧

Must I stand and crouch
Under your testy humor?

❧

10.   Cassius to Brutus (scene iii):

❧

Hath Cassius lived
To be but mirth and laughter to his Brutus,
When grief and blood ill-tempered vexeth him?

❧

© 1993 by The Center for Applied Research in Education

NAME:_____   DATE:_____

Vocabulary Review Quiz
for
Julius Caesar
Act IV

Directions: For each of the italicized words in the sentences below, determine which letter best reflects the use of the word in this context. Place the letter corresponding to your answer in the space to the left of the item number.

_____1. Antony, Lepidus, and Octavius *pricked* the names of those they named as traitors.
In this context, *pricked* means

    A. marked   B. decided   C. eliminated   D. questioned

_____2. *Provender* is commonly stored in a barn.
In this context, *provender* means

    A. farm implements   B. gunpowder   C. dry food for livestock
D. harness and tack

_____3. Brutus and Cassius *levied* their armies.
In this context, *levied* means

    A. raised   B. taxed   C. increased   D. decreased

_____4. Lucilius notices that Cassius greeted him with less familiar *instance* than he used to.
In this context, *instance* means

    A. occurrence   B. presence   C. manners   D. greeting

_____5. Brutus showed his *mettle* by facing Octavius and Antony's army.
In this context, *mettle* means

    A. characteristic temperament   B. abrasive manner   C. courage
D. cowardice

_____6. In Act IV, Cassius feels that Brutus *slighted* him in ordering the death of Lucius Pella.
In this context, *slighted* means

    A. admonished   B. severed   C. treated lightly   D. judged harshly

_____7. The *chastisement* for treason is death.
In this context, *chastisement* means

    A. rein   B. reward   C. excuse   D. punishment

153

_____8. Because of a dream, Calphurnia *fretted* about Caesar going to the Capitol on the Ides of March.
In this context, *fretted* means
A. specified   B. worried about   C. dismissed   D. complained

_____9. Steve was *testy* about having to attend summer school.
In this context, *testy* means
A. displeased   B. defensive   C. excited   D. irritably impatient

_____10. John actually enjoyed *vexing* his sister.
In this context, *vexing* means
A. helping   B. supporting   C. irritating   D. fighting

ACT V

Focusing Activities
for
Julius Caesar
Scenarios for Improvisation
Act V

Directions: Presented below are locations and situations involving characters. Before reading an individual scene, pretend to be one of the characters and act out the situation. Don't worry about speaking like the characters in Shakespeare's play; just try to imagine how you would react to the situation and use your own language. Take a few minutes to discuss with the other performers what you would like to do. Be prepared to act out your scene for others in the class. Afterward, classmates outside your group may want to discuss what they've seen.

scene i. *Scene:* A plain near Philippi.

Characters: Octavius, Antony, Brutus, and Cassius.

Situation: The four men meet before going into battle. Octavius and Cassius are eager for battle. Brutus and Antony are willing to try to talk things out rather than fight. Improvise the dialogue among them.

scene v. *Scene:* The battlefield at Philippi near Brutus' camp.

Characters: Antony and Octavius.

Situation: Antony and Octavius' armies have defeated Brutus and Cassius' forces. As they enter Brutus' camp triumphantly, they learn that both Cassius and Brutus have committed suicide rather than be taken prisoner. Improvise what Octavius might say about Cassius at his funeral. Improvise what Antony might say at Brutus' funeral.

NAME:_____   DATE:_____

Focusing Activities
for
Julius Caesar
Small Group Discussion Questions
Act V

Directions: Before reading scenes in Act V, discuss the questions in small groups. You may want to make notes about your discussion, so you can share them with classmates or refer back to them after you've read the scene.

scene i.   If Octavius and Antony were to meet with Brutus and Cassius before battle, how do you think each would respond at the meeting?

scenes ii and iii.   Now that the battle seems inevitable, how do you interpret the warning of Caesar's ghost to Brutus: "I'll see thee again at Philippi?"

scenes iv and v.   If you were Brutus, why would you continue to fight rather than retreat once Cassius was dead?

Focusing Activities
for
Julius Caesar
Speculation Journal
Act V

Directions: This activity will help you become involved actively with reading the play by helping you to determine a definite purpose for reading. Before you read these scenes in Act V, take a few minutes to respond in writing to the questions below. Don't worry about correct answers here. Use your own experience or what you have read in the play to speculate about what you think will happen. After reading a scene you may find that the characters reacted differently than you thought. Don't worry about these differences; just make note of them because you will have opportunities to share these differences in other activities.

scene i. Based upon what you know about the characters in *Julius Caesar,* if Brutus and Cassius were to meet with Octavius and Antony, how might each man react?

scenes ii
and iii. Based upon the characters of Brutus, Cassius, Antony, and Octavius, whose forces do you think might win the battle and why?

scenes iv
and v. Now that Cassius is dead, how do you think Brutus, Antony, and Octavius will respond to it?

Julius Caesar: Act V Speculation Journal (continued)

After Reading Act V and the entire play: Now that you have finished reading the play, which of your speculations were most accurate? How do you account for them? Which ones were least like the action of the play? Why do you think you speculated as you did?

Prereading Activity
for
Julius Caesar
Vocabulary
Act V

Directions: Shakespeare uses the following words in Act V. The section below provides a brief definition of each word and provides a sentence to illustrate its meaning.

Definitions

scene i

1. **ensign** (n.) a military flag used to identify the nationality or allegiance of troops.
   Example: The merchant ship knew it was in trouble once the captain saw the pirate's *ensign:* the flag with a skull and crossbones on it.

2. **gallant** (adj.) brave, high-spirited.
   Example: The *gallant* knight wore his Queen's token into battle.

scene iii

3. **engender** (v.) to produce or cause.
   Example: Ignorance of other cultures often *engenders* distrust among people.

4. **mis-contrue** (v.) to misunderstand or misinterpret meaning.
   Example: The argument occurred because Betty *misconstrued* my remark about her pitching.

5. **spoil** (v.) to plunder, loot, pillage, or carry off as booty.
   Example: Like Roman soldiers after a battle, the looters *spoiled* the appliance store, carrying off television sets and other electrical appliances.

Prereading Activity
for
Julius Caesar
Plot Summaries
Act V

Directions: To help you better understand and follow Shakespeare's play, read the summary of specific scenes immediately before you begin to read the original. If you get lost during the scene, refer to the summary again.

Act V,
scene i   Months later on the plain near Philippi Octavius and Antony discuss the coming battle with Brutus and Cassius. Octavius will lead the right flank and Antony the left. Antony had thought that Brutus and Cassius would remain in the hills rather than come to the plains to fight. But Antony, knowing these men, knew they would come.

Brutus and Cassius and their friends Lucilius, Tintinius, and Messala come to discuss the battle issues. Octavius wants to start the battle now, but Antony stops him. Nothing is resolved, for Octavius and Antony believe the murder of Julius Caesar to be the cowardly act of traitors. Brutus still defends his actions.

Cassius and Brutus realize that the battle is inevitable. Cassius tells Messala that he feels as forced into battle against Roman armies as Pompey was against Julius Caesar. He also confides that he has seen an omen: at Sardis, two eagles came and landed in the camp and let soldiers feed them by hands. Now the eagles are gone and have been replaced by ravens, crows, and kites, all birds that scavenge on the bodies of the dead after battle.

Brutus and Cassius vow that they will not be taken alive if they lose the battle. As lifelong friends, they bid goodbye.

Act V,
scene ii   Brutus sends Messala to give the orders to fight. His forces oppose Octavius'.

Act V,
scene iii   Cassius tells Tintinius that their forces are winning against Antony's. Cassius himself retrieved his ensign when the standard bearer fled. Tintinius reports that Brutus' forces attacked too soon, overtook Octavius', and then began looting while Antony's forces surrounded Cassius'. Pindarus, Cassius' servant, reports that Antony has taken Cassius' camp, so he must flee.

Cassius asks Tintinius to take Cassius' horse and ride to the camp to investigate. Cassius then asks Pindarus to keep a watch and report

© 1993 by The Center for Applied Research in Education

what is happening. Pindarus sees Tintinius ride into the camp and become surrounded by horsemen and hears them shout for joy. Cassius concludes that Antony's troops have taken his friend Tintinius. Feeling that the battle is lost, Cassius makes one last request of Pindarus who became his slave at a battle in Parthia to hold his sword as he kills himself with it. Pindarus does so and flees rather than be a slave to Antony or Octavius.

Tintinius and Messala come to report that Brutus' forces are overtaking Octavius' while Cassius' are defeating Antony's. They discover Cassius' body and go looking for Pindarus. Messala goes to inform Brutus. Meanwhile, Tintinius explains that it was Cassius' victorious troops, not Antony's, that Pindarus saw surround Tintinius when he rode into Cassius' camp. Brutus enters and eulogizes Cassius before he returns to battle.

Act V, scene iv

During battle, Cato and Lucilius decide to tell Antony's soldiers that they are Cato's son and Brutus. Antony's soldiers, thinking they have taken Brutus, report this to Antony. Antony knows that Lucilius is not Brutus, but that he is a prize captive anyway.

Act V, scene v

In another part of the field, Brutus and his servants are tired of fighting. Brutus asks Clitus to hold his sword, so he can kill himself. Clitus refuses, so Brutus asks Dardanius. Brutus reveals to Volumnius that he has again seen the ghost of Caesar the night before and knows that it's time to die. Before Brutus can get Volumnius to hold the sword, another attack comes. Finally, Brutus turns to Strato and kills himself.

Antony, Octavius, and Messala come too late. Strato tells them that Brutus took his own life. Antony eulogizes Brutus as "the noblest Roman of them all," for Brutus believed to the end that he killed Caesar out of honor while the others killed Caesar out of envy. Antony and Octavius take Brutus' body to Octavius' tent and give him an honorable burial.

163

Class Period:

CHARACTER ASSIGNMENTS FOR ORAL READING GROUPS

Julius Caesar

Session 5: Act V

Characters	Group 1	Group 2	Group 3	Group 4
Octavius, Young Cato, Second Soldier	___	___	___	___
Antony	___	___	___	___
Messenger, Lucilius, First Soldier, Clitus	___	___	___	___
Cassius, Dardanius	___	___	___	___
Brutus	___	___	___	___
Messala	___	___	___	___
Tintinius, Voluminus	___	___	___	___
Pindarus, Strato	___	___	___	___

NAME:_____   DATE:_____

During-reading Activity
for
Julius Caesar
Character Diary 5
Act V, scenes i–v

Directions: Use the space below to record your character's reactions to the events that occur in Act V of *Julius Caesar*. Remember to include a summary of events, explain how your character learned of them, and give your character's reactions to these events. Because the act contains five scenes, you may want to record your character's entries as you read each scene. If you need additional room, use the back of this sheet.

The Personal Diary of

_____
(character's name)

_____, 42 B.C.

_____

_____

_____

_____

_____

_____

_____

_____

_____

_____

_____

_____

_____

_____

_____

_____

During-reading Activity
for
Julius Caesar
Guide to Character Development: Brutus
Act V

Shakespeare reveals his characters in four ways:

- through what the characters say to other characters in dialogue
- through what the characters reveal about their thoughts through long speeches to the audience called *soliloquies*
- through what other characters say about them
- through what they do, their actions

As you read the play, examine the following scenes for what they reveal about Brutus' character and fill in the chart briefly using your own words. If you need more room, use the back of the page.

Scene	What Brutus says, does, or what others say about him	What this reveals about Brutus' character
Act V, scene i Brutus and Cassius meet with Octavius and Antony		
Act V, scene ii Brutus begins the battle		
Act V, scene iii Brutus learns of Cassius' death		
Act V, scene iv Antony's soldiers capture Lucilius		
Act V, scene v Brutus dies		

© 1993 by The Center for Applied Research in Education

During-reading Activity
for
Julius Caesar
Guide to Character Development: Cassius
Act V

Shakespeare reveals his characters in four ways:

- through what the characters say to other characters in dialogue

- through what the characters reveal about their thoughts through long speeches to the audience called *soliloquies*

- through what other characters say about them

- through what they do, their actions

As you read the play, examine the following scenes for what they reveal about Cassius' character and fill in the chart briefly using your own words. If you need more room, use the back of the page.

Scene	What Cassius says, does, or what others say about him	What this reveals about Cassius' character
Act V, scene i Brutus and Cassius meet Antony and Octavius		
Act V, scene iii Cassius kills himself		

During-reading Activity
for
Julius Caesar
Guide to Character Development: Antony
Act V

Shakespeare reveals his characters in four ways:

- ❧ through what the characters say to other characters in dialogue
- ❧ through what the characters reveal about their thoughts through long speeches to the audience called *soliloquies*
- ❧ through what other characters say about them
- ❧ through what they do, their actions

As you read the play, examine the following scenes for what they reveal about Antony's character and fill in the chart briefly using your own words. If you need more room, use the back of the page.

Scene	What Antony says, does, or what others say about him	What this reveals about Antony's character
Act V, scene i Antony, Octavius, Brutus, and Cassius meet		
Act V, scene iv Antony recognizes that Lucilius is not Brutus		
Act V, scene v Antony eulogizes Brutus		

© 1993 by The Center for Applied Research in Education

NAME:_____   DATE:_____

Postreading Activity
for
Julius Caesar
Comprehension Check
Act V

Directions: After you've read all of Act V, use the following questions to check how well you've understood what you've read. For each question, select the most appropriate answer from the choices listed below it. Place the letter corresponding to your answer in the space to the left of the item number.

_____1.   Why do Brutus and Cassius bid each other farewell before the battle begins?

A. They would rather die honorably in battle than be taken prisoner.
B. They plan to meet after the battle.
C. They are brothers-in-law.
D. They have been poisoned.
E. They know that they probably will be defeated.

_____2.   When Cassius sends Tintinius to ride into his camp, Tintinius is surrounded by cheering soldiers. Cassius presumes this means

A. Tintinius has rallied Cassius' troops.
B. Antony's soldiers have taken Cassius' camp.
C. that Tintinius has been killed.
D. that Brutus has led a counterattack against Antony.
E. that Octavius' soldiers have taken Cassius' camp.

_____3.   As a result of Pindarus' report about Tintinius, Cassius

A. orders a counterattack.
B. returns to battle to lead a counterattack.
C. sends a message to Brutus.
D. commits suicide.
E. surrenders to Antony and Octavius.

169

_____4. When Brutus learns what Cassius has done, he immediately

      A. orders Lucilius to take his place.
      B. returns to battle.
      C. sends a letter to Octavius.
      D. commits suicide.
      E. surrenders to Antony and Octavius.

_____5. Whom does Antony call "the noblest Roman of them all"?

      A. Julius Caesar
      B. Octavius
      C. Brutus
      D. Portia
      E. Cassius

NAME:_____   DATE:_____

Postreading Activity
for
Julius Caesar
Small Group Discussion to Check Comprehension
Act V

Directions: After you've read all of Act V, in small groups, or as your teacher directs, discuss each of the following questions briefly. Use the space below each question to note points you may want to share later.

1. What are the positions of Octavius, Antony, Brutus, and Cassius before battle?

2. Why do Brutus and Cassius bid each other an everlasting farewell at the end of scene i?

3. In what ways is Cassius' suicide in keeping with his character throughout the play?

4. Why do Brutus' actions cause Antony to eulogize him as "the noblest Roman of them all"?

Postreading Activity
for
Julius Caesar
Critical Thinking Questions
Act V

Directions: To help develop your understanding of Act V, take time to think about and discuss these questions. The first question is the focus question and the point of the discussion. Don't be concerned that you may not be able to answer it at first. Proceed to the exploration questions and then return to the focus question.

Focus Question. What makes it possible for a person to die today, as Brutus does, for a noble cause?

Exploration Questions.

1. What do you consider are the character traits that make a person "honorable"?

2. What are Antony's reasons for calling Brutus "the noblest Roman of them all"?

3. Why might you believe that our society places little value upon personal honor?

4. Compare Brutus with another honorable character in literature that you've read.

5. Do you agree with Antony's reasons for calling Brutus noble?

6. What criteria do you use to judge whether or not a character in literature is noble?

Postreading Activity
for
Julius Caesar
Language Exploration
Irony of Situation
Act V

Often in works of literature, the author will use *irony of situation*. Irony of situation occurs when a discrepancy exists between what a character says and what a character does, or a discrepancy between what a character expects to happen and what does happen.

For example, in Act I, scene i, Marullus reminds the citizens who are taking the day off from work to cheer Caesar's return from defeating Pompey's sons that they once cheered Pompey's victories. In Act I, scene ii, slow-witted Casca is able to describe in detail how Caesar refused the crown three times. Although it leads the Senate to name Caesar king, Casca doesn't see it as important. Caesar also does not grasp that it is ironic that Calphurnia's dream is a prophecy of his death, but Decius is able to use a more flattering interpretation to lure Caesar to his death.

Directions: The following passages from Acts IV and V are examples of irony of situation. Working in pairs, small groups, or as your teacher directs, review each passage in the context of the play and decide why the situations are ironic.

1. Lepidus consenting to having his brother killed (Act IV, scene i):

    ❧

    Upon condition Publius shall not live,
    Who is your sister's son, Mark Antony.

    ❧

2. Antony commenting upon Lepidus to Octavius (Act IV, scene i):

    ❧

    This is a slight unmeritable man,
    Meet to be sent on errands. Is it fit,
    The threefold world divided, he should stand
    One of the three to share it?

    ❧

173

3.   Brutus to Cassius (Act IV, scene iii):

ॐ

Sheathe your dagger.
Be angry when you will, it shall have scope.
Do what you will, dishonour shall be humour.
O Cassius, you are yoked with a lamb
That carries anger as the flint bears fire
Who much enforce shows a hasty spark,
And straight is cold again.

ॐ

4.   Brutus to Lucius and then to the Ghost of Caesar (Act IV, scene iii):

ॐ

Let me see, let me see; is not the leaf turned down
Where I left reading? Here it is I think,
How ill this taper burns! Ha! Who comes here?
I think it is some weakness of mine eyes
That shapes this monstrous apparition.

ॐ

5.   Cassius to Messala (Act V, scene i):

ॐ

This is my birth-day; as this very day
Was Cassius born.

ॐ

174

6.　Tintinius to Cassius (Act V, scene iii):

O Cassius, Brutus gave the word too early,
Who having some advantage on Octavius,
Took it too eagerly: his soldiers fell to spoil,
Whilst we by Antony are all enclosed.

7.　Pindarus to Cassius (Act V, scene iii):

Tintinius is enclosed round about
With horsemen, that make to him on the spur
Yet he spurs on. Now they are almost on him.

8.　Messala to Tintinius (Act V, scene iii):

It is but change, Tintinius; for Octavius
Is overthrown by noble Brutus' power,
As Cassius legions are by Antony.

9. Brutus (Act V, scene iii):

O Julius Caesar, thou art mighty yet;
Thy spirit walks abroad, and turns our swords
In our own proper entrails.

10. Brutus to the slaves (Act V, scene v):

I shall have glory by this losing day,
More than Octavius and Mark Antony
By this veil conquest shall attain unto.

Language Exploration Review
Julius Caesar

Directions: Now that you've discussed all the Language Exploration Activities, use the following questions to check how well you can apply what you've learned to new selections. For each question, select the most appropriate answer from the choices listed below it. Place the letter corresponding to your answer in the space to the left of the item number.

_____1. The following line is an example of which figurative device?

ᴈ

Rome, thou hast lost the breed of noble bloods

ᴈ

A. simile
B. metaphor
C. symbol
D. apostrophe
E. irony

_____2. When Marullus and Flavius remove the decorations from Caesar's images, their action is

A. a visual image.
B. a symbol of their support of Caesar.
C. a symbol of their defiance of Caesar.
D. a metaphor for government.
E. a model for the Roman senate.

_____3. In the following lines, which sense does the imagery appeal to?

ᴈ

'Tis true, this god did shake,
His coward lips did from their colour fly,
And that same eye, whose bend doth awe the world
Did lose his lustre,

ᴈ

A. sight
B. sound
C. taste
D. touch
E. smell

_____4. The following line is an example of which figurative device?

Let's carve him as a dish fit for the gods

    A. simile
    B. metaphor
    C. symbol
    D. apostrophe
    E. irony

_____5. When Brutus says "not that I loved Caesar less; but that I loved Rome more," it is an example of

    A. verbal irony.
    B. metaphor.
    C. symbol.
    D. irony of situation.
    E. visual imagery.

_____6. What type of figurative device is used in the following lines?

Pardon me Julius! Here wast thou bayed, brave hart;
Here didst thou fall; and here thy hunters stand.

    A. verbal irony
    B. metaphor
    C. symbol
    D. irony of situation
    E. visual imagery

_____7. During the funeral oration, Antony refers to Caesar's will with the following lines:

Will you be patient? Will you stay awhile?
I have o'ershot myself to tell you of it.
I fear I wrong the honorable men,
Whose daggers have stabbed Caesar; I do fear it.

These lines are an example of

A. verbal irony.
B. metaphor.
C. symbol.
D. irony of situation.
E. visual imagery.

_____8.   Which sense do the following lines appeal to?

≈

Stoop Romans, stoop,
And let us bathe our hands in Caesar's blood
Up to the elbows, and besmear our swords.

≈

A. sight
B. sound
C. taste
D. touch
E. smell

_____9.   Which figurative device is used in the following lines to refer to error?

≈

O hateful Error, Melancholy's child,
Why dost thou show to the apt thoughts of men
The things that are not.

≈

A. simile
B. metaphor
C. symbol
D. personification
E. irony

10. In the following lines, how does Brutus view Antony?

ε‌

And for Mark Antony, think not of him;
For he can do no more than Caesar's arm
When Caesar's head is off.

ε‌

A. as a symbol of power
B. as a visual image of death
C. as a symbolic part of Caesar
D. as a metaphor for good government
E. as a traitor to Rome

Postreading Activity
for
Julius Caesar
Vocabulary in Context
Act V

Directions: In each of the passages below you will find one of the words from the prereading vocabulary list for Act V. Review the definitions given in the prereading vocabulary. Working individually, in pairs, or in small groups as your teacher directs, examine each of the underlined words in the following passages from Act V. For each word, use the appropriate meaning and develop a brief interpretation of the passage within the context of the play.

1. Messenger informing Octavius and Antony that Brutus and Cassius' army is approaching (scene i):

ร

The enemy comes on in <u>gallant</u> show.

ร

2. Cassius explaining the two eagles as an omen to Messala (scene i):

ร

Coming from Sardis, on our former <u>ensign</u>
Two eagles fell and there they perched,
Gorging and feeding from our soldier's hands.

ร

181

3. Tintinius explaining why Brutus' troops couldn't help his (scene iii):

&

> *O Cassius, Brutus gave the word too early,*
> *Who having advantage on Octavius,*
> *Took it too eagerly: his soldiers fell <u>to spoil</u>.*

&

4. Messala commenting upon Cassius' death to Tintinius (scene iii):

&

> *O Error soon conceived,*
> *Thou never com'st unto a happy birth,*
> *But kill'st the mother that <u>engendered</u> thee.*

&

5. Messala addressing the dead Cassius (scene iii):

&

> *Alas, thou hast <u>misconstrued</u> everything.*

&

NAME:_____ DATE:_____

Vocabulary Review Quiz
for
Julius Caesar
Act V

Directions: For each of the italicized words in the sentences below, determine which letter best reflects the use of the word in this context. Place the letter corresponding to your answer in the space to the left of the item number.

_____1. The soldiers made a *gallant* showing as they marched off to war.
In this context, *gallant* means
A. high-spirited   B. colorful   C. anxious   D. enthusiastic

_____2. Francis Scott Key knew that Fort McHenry had not been taken when he saw the American *ensign* flying over it at dawn.
In this context, *ensign* means
A. flag   B. officer   C. aircraft   D. eagle

_____3. The army *spoiled* the town after conquering it.
In this context, *spoiled* means
A. rotted   B. plundered   C. overran   D. burned

_____4. A series of misunderstandings *engendered* Cassius' death.
In this context, *engendered* means
A. fostered   B. postponed   C. hastened   D. caused

_____5. Because the student didn't listen carefully, he *misconstrued* the teacher's remarks about his work.
In this context, *misconstrued* means
A. misinterpreted   B. understood   C. challenged   D. repeated

EXTENDING ACTIVITIES

Overview of
Extending Activities
for
Julius Caesar

Directions: Now that you've completed your formal study of *Julius Caesar*, the extending activities listed below will provide you with opportunities to extend your understanding of the play. Remember that these are suggestions of things you might do. Perhaps you will think of others or your teacher may have additional suggestions. Your teacher can provide you with specific sets of directions for **acting out, oral interpretation, paper bag theater, masks,** and **writing assignments**.

Acting Out:

1. Dramatize a missing scene related to the characters and situations in the play. For example, how and when does Brutus tell his wife Portia about his plans?

2. Present a scene from the play in a modern context. Use contemporary settings, words, and ideas. For example, what might Antony's funeral oration be like as a modern political speech or done in rap form?

Oral Interpretation: Present a prepared reading of the speech of a single character, between two characters, or of an entire scene. Keep in mind that oral interpretation involves communicating the words effectively *without* actually memorizing a script and acting out the scene with full costumes and props.

Paper Bag Theater: *Make paper bag puppets and present a scene from the play.*

Masks: Create paper plate masks for specific characters and present a scene from the play wearing them.

Writing Assignments:

1. Write an alternative ending to the play.

2. Research some element of Roman life in the time of Julius Caesar (c. 100–44 B.C.)

3. Using the character diary you kept while reading the play, write a letter or note from your character to another character in the play.

© 1993 by The Center for Applied Research in Education

Visual Displays:

1. Create a graffiti wall for Rome at some specific time during the play.

2. Create a time line for the play where you list the significant events in order.

3. Draw a comic strip or drawing for a scene from the play.

4. Create a filmstrip or video related to the play.

5. Construct a mobile: use double-sided objects/characters from the play with a 3 × 5 card containing a description beneath each object.

6. Create a music video combining still pictures with music and words.

7. Multiple panel quilt: select and depict 12 or 16 scenes from the play. Make each panel out of paper. For each panel of your quilt, create an illustration and write a caption which explains it. Create a border for each panel and tie or string them together to form a large wall hanging.

8. Research and build a Globe Theater model.

9. Research and present samples of Roman cooking.

10. Research and present how Elizabethan actors may have interpreted Roman costumes.

11. Create a slide sound presentation about some aspect of the play.

Extending Activities
for
Julius Caesar
Acting Out

Directions: From time to time during your study of *Julius Caesar,* your teacher may have asked you to participate in an improvised scene from the play. You may have improvised scenes either before or after you read particular scenes. Now that you've read the entire play, here are some additional opportunities for you to act out and demonstrate your fuller understanding of the play and its characters. Either you or your teacher may have additional ideas that will work as well. As your teacher directs, you may wish to improvise these scenes or to fully script and rehearse them.

1. Suppose you are Marullus or Flavius. How do you defend your taking down the decorations from Caesar's statues when you are brought before Julius Caesar?

2. Suppose you were the psychologist to whom Brutus had come during Act I of the play. How would you help him sort out his feelings of ambiguity about Caesar?

3. Immediately following Act I, scene iii, Casca returns home. What might he tell his wife about his day?

4. Sometime between Act III, scene ii (when Antony delivers his funeral oration) and Act IV, scene i (where Antony, Octavius, and Lepidus decide who will be killed to avenge Caesar's death), Antony, Octavius, and Lepidus meet to form the alliance known as the Second Triumvirate. What do they say during their meeting?

5. After the end of the play, Antony appears once before the people of Rome to explain what has happened to Brutus and Cassius and to let them know that he and Octavius now rule Rome. What does he say?

6. Create a scene in the Roman underworld (Tartarus, where the persons of the Earth are imprisoned, or Erebus, where others go) where specific characters defend their lives.

7. Brutus confronts Lucius Pella on the charges of bribery. What does Pella say in his own defense and how does Brutus respond?

8. Portia goes to Calphurnia on the morning of the Ides of March. What do they say to each other?

9. Develop a segment for "60 Minutes," CBS (or NBC or ABC) Evening News, "Entertainment Tonight," "Phil Donahue," "Oprah," "Geraldo," "Now It Can Be Told," or "A Current Affair" based upon *Julius Caesar.*

10. The carpenter and the cobbler from Act I, scene i are in one of their kitchens discussing the events of the day. What would they say after Caesar refuses the crown in Act I, scene ii? How might they react to the strange storm in Acts I and II? After learning that Antony and Octavius have had 100 senators killed? After learning of the defeat of Brutus and Cassius?

Extending Activity
for
Julius Caesar
Oral Interpretation

Directions: One possibility for an extending activity is for you to present a prepared reading of a speech or scene from *Julius Caesar*. Presented below are suggestions of solo and duet scenes that you may wish to present. You may wish to check with your teacher and present other scenes. To help you prepare your scene, work through all the steps.

Solo Scenes:

> Brutus, Act II, scene i—his soliloquy beginning "It must be by his death. . ."
> Brutus, Act III, scene ii—address to the people at Caesar's funeral. Omit the citizens' lines.
> Antony, Act III, scene ii—Antony's funeral oration. Omit the citizens' lines.

Scenes for Two Performers:

> Marullus and Flavius, Act I, scene i—chiding the citizens for forgetting Pompey.
> Brutus and Cassius, Act I, scene ii—discussion of Caesar's growing power.
> Cicero and Casca, Act I, scene iii—discussion of the storm.
> Cassius and Casca, Act I, scene iii—discussion of the storm and Caesar.
> Brutus and Portia, Act II, scene i—her inquiring what's bothering him.
> Caesar and Calphurnia, Act II, scene ii—discussion of her dream and the omens.
> Portia and the Soothsayer, Act II, scene iv—her inquiring about the welfare of Caesar.
> Antony and Octavius, Act IV, scene i—discussion of Lepidus.
> Brutus and Cassius, Act IV, scene iii—quarrel.
> Brutus and Cassius, Act V, scene i—farewell.

Steps for Preparing an Oral Interpretation:

1. Select a scene or passage that you really like. The passage should have a definite beginning, high point, and an end. Remember that you will be doing a prepared reading and not memorizing a script. Most often oral interpreters either stand before their audience or sit on a stool.

2. Prepare a script to work from. You may want to type out the selection or Xerox it from a book. You'll need a copy that you can make notes on. Mount your script on black construction paper, so you can read from it easily without having to hold it with both hands. Keep the

pages of your manuscript loose, so you can either slide them out of the way or shift them under each other as you finish reading them.

3. Analyze the script. As you work through the analysis, make notes to yourself in pencil on your script.

    a. Read the whole passage and decide what it's about. Because you've already read the whole play, you know where your selection fits into the development of the characters.

    b. Read the whole piece several times and decide what the overall effect of the piece is.

    c. Make notes of things you don't understand—allusions, words, and so forth. Check the footnotes in your text or look up unfamiliar words in the dictionary. Remember that the meaning of particular words may have changed since Shakespeare's time. If you have a problem understanding a particular word, check the glossary of terms found in most editions of Shakespeare's plays in your library.

    d. As you look at individual words, you should know how to pronounce all of them as well as knowing both their denotative meaning (the dictionary meaning) and their connotative meaning (the emotional subtleties that come from using the word in a particular context).

    e. Where does the scene take place? Is it a public place, like the streets of Rome, or a private one, like Brutus' garden or inside his tent? Who speaks here and what is the speaker's emotional state at the time? What has happened before this scene?

    f. Examine the overall organization of the scene. What emotions do the characters reveal in this scene? What changes in character, motivation, or emotions occur during the scene? For example, in Antony's funeral oration, Antony shifts his topics slightly, moving from Caesar's ambition, to his will, to revealing the body, to stirring civil unrest. Decide how you can convey these changes with your voice.

4. Begin practicing aloud. Read the passage out loud, either working with a partner or with a tape recorder. Listen to yourself. Experiment with different readings. Underline words you wish to emphasize. Make marginal notes about the emotions you wish to portray in different parts.

5. Write a brief introduction to your scene, setting it up for your listeners. The following example could be used to introduce Act II, scene i.

Once Brutus consents to join the conspiracy against Caesar, Cassius and the others leave. In the stillness of his orchard in the hours before dawn, Brutus' wife Portia confronts her husband about his unusual behavior during the past few days.

6. Once you've decided on how you wish to read your selection, practice, practice, practice! Your goal in these sessions is not to memorize the words but to learn the interpretation, so that when you present it, you can concentrate on a smooth performance.

7. Perform the piece. Some interpreters wish to stand while others wish to sit on stools. You may hold your script in your hands or use a music stand or lectern.

Extending Activity
for
Julius Caesar
Paper Bag Theater

One way to present scenes from *Julius Caesar* without having to worry about elaborate sets or costumes is to use puppets made from brown paper bags. You can make your own puppets using construction paper, scissors, rubber cement, crayons, and felt tip markers. You can use a table turned sideways as a stage for the puppeteers to hide behind. If you feel that you need scenery, make a mural and use masking tape to secure it to the wall behind you.

*Steps to Making
and Performing Scene
with Puppets:*

1. Select a scene that you want to perform. Listed below are scenes for two, three, or more actors.

*Scenes for
Two Actors:* Marullus and Flavius, Act I, scene i—chiding the citizens for forgetting Pompey.
Brutus and Cassius, Act I, scene ii—discussion of Caesar's growing power.
Cicero and Casca, Act I, scene iii—discussion of the storm.
Cassius and Casca, Act I, scene iii—discussion of the storm and Caesar.
Brutus and Portia, Act II, scene i—her inquiring what's bothering him.
Caesar and Calphurnia, Act II, scene ii—discussion of her dream and the omens.
Portia and the Soothsayer, Act II, scene iv—her inquiring about the welfare of Caesar.
Antony and Octavius, Act IV, scene i—discussion of Lepidus.
Brutus and Cassius, Act IV, scene iii—quarrel.
Brutus and Cassius, Act V, scene i—farewell.

*Scenes for
Three or
More Perfor-
mers:* Flavius, Marullus, First Citizen (carpenter), Second Citizen (cobbler), Act I, scene i—the tribunes chide the citizens for cheering Caesar's victory.
Brutus, Cassius, Casca, Cinna, Metellus, Decius, Trebonius, Act II, scene i—plotting the assassination.
Caesar, Calphurnia, Decius, Act II, scene ii—Decius convinces Caesar to go to the Capitol.
Portia, Lucius, Soothsayer, Act II, scene iv—Portia fears for the safety of Brutus.

© 1993 by The Center for Applied Research in Education

Decius, Brutus, Cinna, Caesar, Metellus, Cassius, Casca Act III, scene i—assassination of Caesar.

Antony, Brutus, Cassius, Act III, scene i—Brutus and Cassius agree to permit Antony to speak at Caesar's funeral.

Brutus, Lucilius, Pindarus, Act IV, scene ii—Pindarus tells Brutus of Cassius' anger over Brutus' treatment of Lucius Pella.

2. Design and make puppets. In making your puppets refer to *Figure 1*. To make your puppet talk, insert your hand into the bag and curl your fingers so the top of the bag with the upper face on it moves up and down.

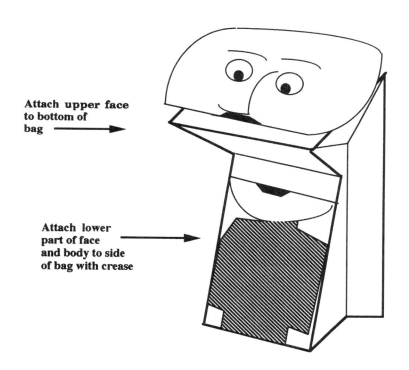

Attach upper face to bottom of bag →

Attach lower part of face and body to side of bag with crease →

Figure 1
Paper Bag Puppet

3. Prepare your script as if you were doing an oral interpretation. See specific directions entitled Extending Activity for *Julius Caesar:* Oral Interpretation.

4. Decide how you can make your puppet appear to walk and move.

5. Practice, practice, practice.

Extending Activity
for
Julius Caesar
Paper Plate Masks

Directions: One way to help you present scenes from *Julius Caesar* is to create a half-mask to represent the character of a specific scene. When you present your scene, hold the mask in front of you and create the character.

To make your own mask, you will need:

large white paper plates (do not use plastic plates)
large craft stick
scissors
glue (either rubber cement or hot melt glue gun work well)
assorted construction paper, ribbon, cloth, cardboard, yarn to make hair, hats and other decorations that help represent the character
crayons, colored pencils, and felt-tip markers

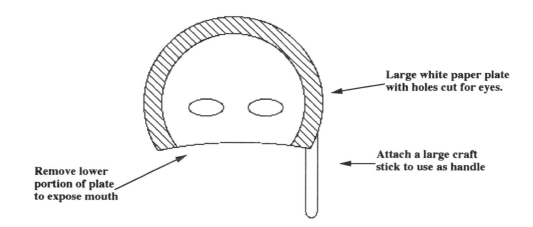

Large white paper plate with holes cut for eyes.

Attach a large craft stick to use as handle

Remove lower portion of plate to expose mouth

Figure 2
Paper Plate Mask

Extending Activities
for
Julius Caesar
Writing Assignments

Directions: Given below are some ideas for possible writing assignments based upon your understanding of the characters and situations in *Julius Caesar*.

1. You are the casting director for a new film version of *Julius Caesar*. Write a letter to the film's producers explaining who from among current film, television, or rock and roll stars you would like to cast in each of the play's principal roles: Brutus, Cassius, Mark Antony, Caesar, Octavius, Portia, and Calphurnia.

2. Write Portia's letter of farewell to Brutus.

3. Write a new or more satisfying ending to the play.

4. Create a "Meeting of Minds" where characters from *Julius Caesar* interact with characters from literature. You may also want to have the characters interact with their authors.

5. Create a children's version of the play. Check *Shake Hands with Shakespeare* or Charles and Caroline Lamb's *Tales from Shakespeare*.

6. Create an illustrated children's book based upon *Julius Caesar*.

7. Write Antony's funeral oration for Marcus Brutus.

8. Investigate the Globe Theater restoration project in London and report your findings to the class.

9. Research the food, clothing, housing, festivals, or celebrations for either Elizabethan England or Rome during the time of Julius and Augustus Caesar.

10. Using the character diary that you kept during your reading of the play, write a letter to your cousin in Athens relaying both the events of the play and your response to them.

11. As one of the characters in the play, write a letter to either "Dear Abby" or "Ann Landers" and the columnist's reply.

12. Research the development and historical aspect of weapons used at the time of Caesar or in Shakespeare's time.

PART THREE

Appendices

Appendix A

EVALUATING READING PROCESS ACTIVITIES

This section serves three purposes:

- to suggest means to incorporate the evaluation of reading process activities into a grade for a unit on *Julius Caesar;*

- to explain how to set up and review reading activity folders;

- to review the instructional goals for the activities in this resource and to suggest specific guidelines for evaluating them.

INCORPORATING READING PROCESS ACTIVITY WITHIN A UNIT ON JULIUS CAESAR

With a reading workshop approach to literature, just as with a writing workshop approach to written composition, the teacher has to decide how to assess students' participation in process activities as well as to evaluate the formal products that demonstrate learning. The activities in this resource provide opportunities for students to improve their reading, writing, speaking, listening, and critical thinking processes as well as learn about *Julius Caesar.* Although you don't need to grade all the process activities formally, you will want to review and respond to your students' work as they read the play. If you and your students were to devote two to three weeks to a unit on *Julius Caesar,* you might use the percentages listed in the table below.

SUGGESTED COMPONENTS OF UNIT GRADE

Activity	Percentage of Unit Grade	Numbers of Items and Point Values	Total
Prereading activities	5%	(5 reading sessions @ 5 pts.)	25 pts.
Response journals or character diaries	25%	(5 [one per act] @ 25 pts.)	125 pts.
Postreading activities	10%	(5 summary sessions @ 10 pts.)	50 pts.
Comprehension checks	10%	(5 @ 10 pts.)	50 pts.
Vocabulary review quizzes	10%	(5 @ 10 pts.)	50 pts.
Language exploration activities	10%	(5 @ 10 pts.)	50 pts.
Language exploration review quiz	5%		25 pts.
Individual or group extending activity	25%		125 pts.
Total	**100%**		**500 pts.**

SETTING UP AND REVIEWING READING ACTIVITY FOLDERS

Reading folders allow the students to keep their prereading, during-reading, and postreading activities together for the entire unit. Any type of folder works well although two pocket folders allow storage of response journals or character diaries on one side and other reading process activities on the opposite side.

To monitor students' progress and to provide formative evaluation, review approximately 20 percent of the students' folders for each class period at the end of each day. Select the folders at random, so the class doesn't know when you will check any individual's work. Take a few minutes to skim and scan the work in each folder.

As you review each student's work, check to see that the student understands the directions and purpose of each activity. Use brief comments to praise the work specifically and to point out certain deficiencies. Then record the date of your review and any point values. You might try using + √ for outstanding work, √ for satisfactory work, and —√ for less than satisfactory work because students may find these symbols less threatening than traditional letter grades. You can translate codes like these into a numerical equivalent for your records: for example, awarding 5 points for outstanding work, 4 for satisfactory, and 3 for less than satisfactory.

INSTRUCTIONAL GOALS AND EVALUATIVE GUIDELINES
FOR SPECIFIC READING ACTIVITIES

This section states both the instructional goals for specific reading process activities and suggests possible ways to assess them.

Focusing Activities

Although students complete only *one* focusing activity for a particular scene, all focusing activities share two common *instructional goals:*

ಇ to help students use prior knowledge related to *Julius Caesar;*

ಇ to establish a purpose for reading a scene.

Scenarios for Improvisation

Guidelines for Assessment:

Does the student

ಇ actively participate as either actor or audience?

ಇ provide logical motivations for the character's actions?

ಇ establish actions that are consistent with the setting and existing information about the character?

Prereading Discussion Questions

Guidelines for Assessment:

Does the student

- ✌ participate in discussion?

- ✌ share ideas willingly?

- ✌ allow others to share ideas?

- ✌ provide explanation or support for ideas?

- ✌ provide speculations that are consistent with the student's existing knowledge of *Julius Caesar?*

Speculation Journal

Guidelines for Assessment:

Does the student

- ✌ address the issues contained in the question(s)?

- ✌ provide explanation or support for ideas?

- ✌ provide speculations that are consistent with the student's existing knowledge of *Julius Caesar?*

Introducing the Play with Videotape

Guidelines for Assessment:

Does the student

- ✌ attempt to answer all questions?

- ✌ address the issues in the questions?

- ✌ have an overall understanding of the scene and its conflict?

Vocabulary

Instructional Goals:

- ✌ to review definitions of less familiar words

- ✌ to demonstrate the effect of context upon meaning

Plot Summaries

Instructional Goals:

- ✌ to establish an overview of each scene

- ✌ to provide a reference for the student when Shakespeare's text seems incomprehensible

Response Journals

As one of two ongoing writing-to-learn activities that students may use during their reading of *Julius Caesar,* the response journal has two *instructional goals:*

✌ to summarize and reflect upon the meaning of the play

✌ to recognize, record, and comment upon repeated elements found in the play, such as *symbols, motifs, themes, character development,* or *figurative language*

Guidelines for Assessment:

Does the student

✌ record an entry for each reading session?

✌ meet minimum length requirements for each entry?

✌ respond emotionally, associatively, figuratively?

✌ demonstrate an accurate understanding of the literary facts of *Julius Caesar?*

✌ demonstrate an honest effort to begin making sense of the play and developing an understanding of it?

✌ probe responses and attempt to understand them rather than summarize or paraphrase the action of the play?

Character Diary

As one of two ongoing writing-to-learn activities that students may use during their reading of *Julius Caesar,* the character diary has two *instructional goals:*

✌ to summarize and reflect upon the meaning of the play

✌ to begin to evaluate the action of the play from the perspective of an individual character

Guidelines for Assessment:

Does the student

✌ record an entry for each reading session?

✌ meet minimum length requirements for each entry?

✌ provide an account for how the character learns of the action of the scene(s) just read?

✌ demonstrate an accurate understanding of the literary facts of *Julius Caesar?*

✌ demonstrate an honest effort to begin making sense of the play and developing an understanding of it?

✌ probe responses and attempt to understand them rather than only summarize or paraphrase the action of the play?

Viewing a Scene on Videotape

Unlike using a scene to introduce *Julius Caesar,* viewing a scene after students have read it provides additional information that may help them understand the text of the play.

Instructional Goals:

- to recognize that the performance of a scene affects the student's understanding, comprehension, and interpretation of it;

- to compare and contrast a student's interpretation of a scene with the performers'.

Guidelines for Assessment:

Does the student

- attempt to answer all questions?

- address the issues in the questions?

- demonstrate an honest effort to make sense of the presentation?

- begin to make connections between the videotaped presentation and the text of *Julius Caesar?*

Guides to Character Development

Although students complete these activities after they've read each act, they will reread and contemplate specific portions of the play actively. The students may examine Antony, Brutus, and Cassius as major characters and Julius Caesar and Portia as minor ones.

Instructional Goals:

- to recognize and identify means that Shakespeare uses to develop or reveal character;

- to use evidence from the play to develop and support an interpretation of a character.

Guidelines for Assessment:

Does the student

- attempt to answer all the questions?

- address the issues in the questions?

- use information from the play to develop and support logical conclusions about character(s)?

Comprehension Checks

Both the Comprehension Check and the Small Group Discussion Questions provide means to assess the student's reading comprehension.

Comprehension Checks (Multiple Choice)

Instructional Goal:

◆ to assess reading comprehension of an entire act through factual, interpretative, and evaluative questions.

Guidelines for Assessment:

◆ answer keys appear in the appendix.

Small Group Discussion Questions

Instructional Goal:

◆ to assess reading comprehension of an entire act through factual, interpretative, and evaluative questions.

Guidelines for Assessment:

Does the student

◆ participate in discussion?

◆ attempt to answer all the questions?

◆ address the issues in the questions?

◆ use information from the play to develop and support logical conclusions about the play?

Critical Thinking Questions

Instructional Goals:

◆ to connect the play to the student's life in meaningful ways;

◆ to evaluate interpretations of the play using textual evidence, personal experience, and knowledge of related literature.

Guidelines for Assessment:

Does the student

◆ attempt to answer both the exploration questions as well as the focus question?

◆ address the issues of each question appropriately?

◆ use specific information to support ideas?

◆ integrate personal experience, knowledge of related literature, and textual evidence?

✿ draw logical conclusions from existing evidence?

Language Exploration Activities

Instructional Goals:

✿ to review definitions of selected literary devices and examine them within the context of *Julius Caesar*.

✿ to combine knowledge of literary devices with textual evidence to develop and evaluate interpretations of specific passages of *Julius Caesar*.

Guidelines for Assessment:

Suggested answers appear in the appendix.

Does the student

✿ complete the items that the teacher assigns?

✿ make an effort to apply the definition of the literary device to the lines in the play?

✿ review the passage within the broader context of the individual speech, scene, or play?

✿ provide specific support of interpretation(s)?

Language Exploration Review Quiz

Instructional Goal:

✿ to assess the student's understanding of how specific literary devices affect the interpretation of specific passages from *Julius Caesar*.

Guidelines for Assessment:

An answer key appears in the appendix.

Has the student

✿ completed the preceding language exploration activities?

Vocabulary in Context

Instructional Goals:

✿ to review the additional meanings of words;

✿ to analyze the use of specific words within the context of a particular passage;

✿ to develop interpretations of specific passages using knowledge and context.

Guidelines for Assessment:

Suggested answers appear in the appendix.

Does the student

❧ complete the items that the teacher assigns?

❧ review the definitions of the words?

❧ make an effort to apply the meaning of the word to the lines in the play?

❧ review the passage within the broader context of the individual speech, scene, or play?

❧ provide specific support of interpretation(s)?

Vocabulary Review Quizzes

Instructional Goal:

❧ to assess the student's understanding of specific words in context.

Guidelines for Assessment:

Answers appear in the appendix.

Has the student

❧ reviewed the meaning of the words?

❧ completed the preceding vocabulary in context activities?

Individual or Group Extending Activities

Instructional Goals:

❧ to apply knowledge and understanding of *Julius Caesar* to new situations and contexts.

❧ to provide additional opportunities for students to apply reading, writing, speaking, listening, viewing, and critical thinking skills.

Guidelines for Assessment:

Do the students

❧ have a purpose and focus for their extending activities that are related to the play and the study of it directly?

❧ present information clearly and logically?

❧ present information, whether from the play or research, accurately and with appropriate documentation?

❧ present interpretations of characters or events from the play that are consistent with the information in the text?

❧ meet all appropriate additional criteria and specifications that the teacher has set?

MEANS FOR CHECKING STUDENTS'
COMPREHENSION OF TEXT

When I review students' responses to reading process activities, I can determine whether they understand the reading quickly. Written quizzes aren't the only way to check their comprehension. Here are several others:

1. Skim through the response journal and pay attention to the emotional and figurative responses.

2. Review the character diaries, looking for an accurate understanding of events. Literacy facts recorded in either response journals or character diaries should be accurate. For example, students should state that Brutus, not Cassius, speaks first at Caesar's funeral.

3. Allow students to improvise with their own language the action of the scene they have just read. As the student actors get stuck, allow other students either to side coach the actors or to replace them at a particular moment. The purpose of this activity is to promote comprehension of what the students have just read. When questions arise, mediate and direct the students back to Shakespeare's text for support. Ask some variation of "How do you know? where does the text indicate your point?"

4. Allow students to improvise the scenes using simple masks, stick puppets, or paper bag puppets.

5. Have students turn their books face down and try to write brief summaries until they get stuck. Allow them to look at the text again before continuing.

Appendix B

USING SMALL GROUPS SUCCESSFULLY

I advocate using small groups throughout this resource. Small groups are a great way to get lots of students involved quickly. The following practices make these groups operate more effectively:

- Assign students to specific groups. When they self-select their groups, they may socialize rather than focus on the task at hand.

- Mix students of different backgrounds, abilities, and talents. In discussion situations, multiple perspectives often lead to insights.

- Structure the group assignments and provide written directions (on the chalkboard, overhead projector, or in written handouts). When students know their audience and the purpose of the assignment, they tend to stay on task. All members of the group need to understand what their jobs are, what the final product needs to look like, and how much time they have to complete it.

- Establish class rules for small group behavior and encourage students to work together.

- Monitor students' behavior as they work in groups. Move around the room in a random fashion.

211

Appendix C

ANSWER KEYS
Comprehension Checks

<table>
<tr><td>

Act I

1.   D
2.   B
3.   C
4.   A
5.   D

</td><td>

Act II

1.   E
2.   B
3.   D
4.   A
5.   B

</td><td>

ACT III

1.   C
2.   E
3.   A
4.   B
5.   C

</td></tr>
</table>

<table>
<tr><td>

Act IV

1.   A
2.   B
3.   C
4.   B
5.   E

</td><td>

Act V

1.   A
2.   B
3.   D
4.   B
5.   C

</td></tr>
</table>

SUGGESTED ANSWERS TO SMALL GROUP DISCUSSION QUESTIONS FOR CHECKING COMPREHENSION

Act I

1. The common people wish to share in Caesar's triumph over Pompey's sons. Caesar brings another victory home to Rome. Flavius and Marullus castigate the crowd for turning against Pompey so easily. They remind the crowd how they once cheered Pompey's victories too. The tribunes' decision to remove the scarves from Caesar's statues suggests that Caesar does not have universal support in Rome.

2. Caesar grudgingly refuses the crown that Antony offers him three times. With each refusal, the crowd cheers louder for Caesar.

3. Caesar characterizes Cassius as having "a lean and hungry look" and one who "thinks too much." Caesar would prefer to have jolly, fat men around him who show their emotions and thoughts openly rather than the cautious and brooding Cassius.

4. Cassius points out Caesar's mortality. Cassius once rescued Caesar from drowning. Cassius also has seen Caesar succumb to a fever as well as have an epileptic seizure. Cassius also points out that Caesar, like Brutus and

Cassius, was once a noble man but now is greedy for power and wants to be king.

5. ~~Cicero marvels in the storm, calling it wonderful.~~ Although Cicero admits the storm may be ominous, he also acknowledges that humankind will only misinterpret the signs to support beliefs. Casca is afraid of the storm and perceives it as an evil omen.

Act II

1. In his soliloquy, Brutus ponders not what Caesar has done that is tyrannical but what he might do as king or dictator. He concludes that Caesar is dangerous because if he gains any more power, he might abuse it.

2. Brutus points out that the assassination is for the greater good of Rome, it will preserve the Roman Republic. Murdering Antony will make the conspiracy seem too intent on killing and less intent upon preserving ideals.

3. Calphurnia has had her dream of Caesar's statue spouting blood three times during the night of the storm. She also points to omens, similar to those Casca cites earlier to Cicero: a lioness that has given birth in the streets, graves that have opened, the storm, and the "blood on the Capitol."

4. Decius presents an alternative interpretation of Calphurnia's dream. The statue pouring blood must mean that all Romans share in Caesar's victories and greatness. Decius also appeals to Caesar's vanity and manliness asking whether he should go and tell the Senate, "you can't confer the title on Caesar because his wife says he can't come today."

5. Although Portia asks others about Caesar's welfare, she is concerned for her husband. Presumably, Brutus has told her of his plan before going to accompany Caesar to the Senate.

Act III

1. Almost immediately after stabbing Caesar, Brutus says that "ambition's debt is paid." Caesar's death benefits all Romans, for now no one need live in fear of Caesar. He killed Caesar to maintain the liberty, peace, and freedom of all Roman citizens.

2. Brutus speaks before Antony. When Antony does speak, he cannot place blame on the conspirators, and he can only praise Caesar's accomplishments.

3. The effect of Antony's speech is exactly the opposite of his words. In the opening line, Antony comes "to bury Caesar, not to praise him." Actually, Antony does end up praising Caesar's accomplishments later. Although Antony calls Brutus an "honorable man" repeatedly, the repetition and its contexts suggest Brutus is less than honorable.

4. The death of Cinna, the poet, shows that Antony has succeeded in turning the common person against the conspiracy. There's rioting in the streets and senseless mob violence.

Act IV

1. They list names of conspirators and plan to have them killed. These conspirators include Lepidus' brother and Antony's nephew. Octavius and Antony are also willing to make a convenient alliance with Lepidus because he can help them defeat Brutus and Cassius in battle.

2. Cassius defended Lucius Pella for taking bribes in a letter to Brutus. But Brutus ignored Cassius' defense. Cassius feels his character should not be attacked by his friend (and brother-in-law) Brutus.

3. Brutus points out that Caesar was murdered out of noble motives and the conspirators need to remain noble if they are to survive. Brutus feels that a friend should point out his friend's faults. If he doesn't, who will?

4. Portia swallows fire—a painful death that she endures without a sound. This suggests Portia as being a stoic, one who can remain unmoved by extremes of emotion. According to Shakespeare's historical source, Plutarch, Portia did swallow fire. This stoic Portia seems different from the concerned wife in Act II, scene iv.

Act V

1. Cassius and Antony are eager to fight. Brutus wishes to try reasoning once more and reminds Antony and Octavius of his honorable motives. Antony is reasonable at first until Brutus speaks. Once the talking has failed, the battle proves inevitable.

2. Brutus and Cassius vow to die honorably rather than be taken prisoner by Octavius and Antony. If taken prisoner, they know they will be paraded through the streets of Rome as slaves.

3. Cassius seems to react impulsively rather than rationally. Rather than waiting to see why Tintinius was surrounded by a cheering crowd, he presumes it was because Octavius' forces had overtaken his camp. Fearing all is lost, he kills himself by falling on his sword.

4. As Antony points out, the others killed Caesar for personal gain. Brutus always held he did it for the overall good of society.

SUGGESTED ANSWERS FOR LANGUAGE EXPLORATION ACTIVITIES

Act I: Review of Figurative Language

1. Marullus personifies the River Tiber, allowing it to tremble.

2. The metaphor compares Caesar to a soaring bird such as an eagle.

3. In this metaphor, Cassius offers to be a mirror for Brutus.

4. In this simile, Cassius compares himself to Aeneas, mythical founder of Rome who carried his father from Troy as it burned.

5. Here Cassius uses an apostrophe, for he speaks to Brutus after Brutus has left.

6. In this simile, Casca compares the light of the slave's burning hand to the light of twenty torches.

7. In this simile, Cassius compares the unnamed Caesar to the stormy night that Casca fears.

8. Apostrophe. Cassius calls upon the pantheon of Roman gods.

9. Cassius personifies life as a prisoner unable to free himself.

10. Cassius' metaphor compares Caesar to the wolf that preys upon the sheep of Rome who cannot or will not save themselves.

Act II: Symbol

1. The date (March 15) symbolizes the events that will occur that day—Caesar's death.

2. For Caesar, fat men symbolize jolliness and openness of manner and mind. Cassius is the opposite: inward, pensive, brooding.

3. For Casca, the storm symbolizes the gods' discontent among themselves or with humankind.

4. Both of Cassius' metaphors compare Caesar to beasts of prey. Together these symbols portray Caesar as an opportunistic predator because the Roman people are willing to be his prey.

5. Making Caesar kind will likely make him as dangerous as a poisonous adder.

6. Brutus' metaphor makes Caesar the head of the body politic, or the political body of Rome. Symbolically, Antony is an arm of a headless body. With Caesar dead, Antony is harmless.

7. Calphurnia sees these occurrences as omens. The blood dripping from the Capitol symbolizes and foreshadows Caesar's bloody assassination on the steps of the Capitol building.

8. All these images relate to death—both Caesar's death and the death of the Roman Republic that comes with it.

9. Calphurnia sees the storm symbolizing the death of a great prince— Caesar.

10. Caesar's statue symbolizes his power as the Roman state. The spouts are his wounds.

Act III: Verbal Irony

1. Although Cassius compares Caesar to the Colossus of Rhodes, one of the Seven Wonders of the Ancient World, he uses the image to incite Brutus to join the conspiracy.

2. Cassius is falsely modest of his rhetorical skills.

3. Casca doesn't realize the importance of watching Caesar refuse the crown and demonstrate his support among the people. The senators present see Caesar's public support as the will of the people and decide to offer him the crown the next day.

4. The irony here is that Casca doesn't speak Greek, but uses the term "it was Greek to me" to express his inability to comprehend.

5. Cassius is anything but honest as he plots to assassinate Caesar.

6. Although men wore daggers from their belts customarily, here Cassius means to wear his within a wound of Caesar.

7. Calphurnia's interpretation is correct. Decius' flattering interpretation leads Caesar to his death.

8. Caesar welcomes those who will kill him.

9. Antony keeps this bargain but succeeds in turning the people against Brutus and Cassius.

10. Throughout the speech, Antony repeats this phrase raising the question of Brutus' honorable intentions in killing Caesar. In the end, the crowd no longer considers Brutus or any of his followers to be either noble or honorable.

Act IV: Imagery

1. This visual image of the stars and sky equates Caesar with the apparently fixed point of the North Star. It also suggests Caesar considers himself celestial or divine.

2. This grisly visual image draws attention to Caesar's wounds.

3. This image is both visual and sound based. Visually, the stab wounds are compared to open mouths. In terms of sound, these mouths want to speak but can't, so Antony speaks for them as they cry out for revenge.

4. In calling for vengeance, Antony appeals to both smell and sight. Shakespeare evokes images of the smell of dead bodies on the battlefield. Similarly, the visual image is of writhing soldiers as carrion for vultures.

5. Here, the strong visual image is of Lepidus, as the beast of burden.

6. This image appeals to touch.

7. This is another image relating to touch.

8. This image appeals to the sound of a dog howling at the moon.

9. This image appeals to either touch or sound, for the wind can be both felt and heard.

10. The repeated visual images indicate sailing.

Act V: Irony of Situation

1. We expect people to protect, not murder their families.

2. The expectation is that Antony would support his ally, Lepidus, rather than plan to get rid of him.

3. These lines bring the quarrel to a close. The irony of the quarrel is that if Cassius and Brutus cannot maintain their alliance, then they would have no chance of defeating Antony and Octavius.

4. After the quarrel with Cassius, Brutus has calmed down for the night. The song has relaxed him and now he begins to read a book. Just when he should be able to sleep, the ghost appears and disturbs Brutus.

5. Birthdays celebrate a person's life. Cassius dies on the day he should be celebrating his life, not ending it.

6. Cassius believes that both he and Brutus have lost the battle.

7. Cassius believes Pindarus has been captured rather than rallying the troops.

8. Messala brings word of victory just after Cassius has killed himself out of despair.

9. Brutus recognizes the meaning of the ghost's warning. Ironically, Brutus and Cassius defeat themselves, for they've both won the battle militarily.

10. Brutus' glory is in his losing the battle and being able to keep his pledge to Cassius to end his own life rather than be taken prisoner. Antony and Octavius do win but they lose the glory of taking the prize prisoners.

LANGUAGE EXPLORATION REVIEW

1.	D
2.	C
3.	A
4.	A
5.	D
6.	B
7.	A
8.	D
9.	D
10.	C

SUGGESTED ANSWERS FOR
VOCABULARY IN CONTEXT

With all these exercises, encourage students to discuss their ideas and interpretations, for their answers will vary. These are suggestions and shouldn't be interpreted as the only valid responses.

Act I

1. Here, as elsewhere in the scene, Flavius scolds the working men and treats them as being stupid. Literally, Flavius points out that they are manual workers and are supposed to wear their work clothes on a working day.

2. Marullus reminds the Citizens that they once climbed all sorts of structures, including battlements, so they could cheer a victorious Pompey (whom Caesar has just defeated). The types of architectural features that Marullus mentions are typically English rather than Roman.

3. Here *vulgar* refers to *vulgar people* or peasants, not to crude behavior necessarily.

4. Caesar states a superstition that barren women may be cured of their sterility if they are touched during the footrace at the Lupercalia celebrations.

5. Caesar asks the Soothsayer to separate himself from the crowd.

6. Brutus suggests that his troubles are within himself, not from some outside source.

7. These are great thoughts in Cassius' estimation.

8. Cicero, a stoic who accepts many things, suggests that humankind interprets strange happenings according to what it understands. Cicero also suggests that these interpretations may be wrong. Cicero would prefer to just marvel at them.

9. Here's a reference to a classical and medieval belief in a divinely ordered universe. Cassius suggests to Casca that the strange happenings and omens reflect that the world is out of order.

10. Cassius suggests that both Casca and Cinna have estimated Brutus' influence with the Roman people accurately.

Act II

1. As Brutus thinks about what Cassius has told him, he contemplates the dangers of joining the conspiracy and is guarded appropriately.

2. For Brutus, Caesar's increasing power has created a need for serious action.

3. This statement is Brutus' recognition that all of the men are the group of conspirators.

4. Brutus comments upon how Cassius is staring into the night, knowing that Cassius' thoughts are between him and what he is looking at.

5. Caesar points out that his wife has cried out three times in her sleep. Calphurnia's dream seems to take on greater significance because it occurs three times.

6. Caesar wants to face his death directly and courageously rather than hide cowardly from it over and over.

7. Ironically, Calphurnia asks to win while she's on her knees begging.

8. Caesar suggests that Calphurnia sees the omens as being more serious than he does.

9. Artemidorus suggests that the conspirators may be doing what the Fates have already decided for Caesar.

10. Portia compares the swiftness of a rumor being spread to how quickly the sound of a riot can be heard across the city.

Act III

1. Cassius wants the various people who are respectfully asking favors to do so formally at the Capitol.

2. Popilius seems to know of the plans to assassinate Caesar and sees them as a worthy enterprise.

3. Caesar suggests that he and the senate, which he controls, can remedy almost any wrong.

4. Caesar tells Publius Cimber that he is steadfast in his decision not to allow Cimber's brother to return from exile.

5. Brutus suggests to the people that they should judge him more carefully because he has a reputation for being honorable.

6. Brutus again defends himself, suggesting that he is not underestimating Caesar's many accomplishments.

7. Brutus formally begs the crowd to stay and listen to Antony.

8. Antony uses *grievous* in two ways here. First, as causing grief to others and then suggesting that Caesar endured great physical suffering himself in being stabbed repeatedly.

9. Antony is suggesting that Caesar's will, which he probably hasn't seen, has legally given money and property to the citizens of Rome.

10. Although Antony suggests that some may want a physical token as a legacy, he's also implying that Caesar's greatness is also a legacy to the Romans.

Act IV

1. Octavius, Antony, and Lepidus are marking the list of names with dots, much as we'd use a check mark.

2. Octavius rewards his horse with common feed when he does his job.

3. Antony implies that Brutus and Cassius are raising both armies and political support.

4. Literally, Lucilius' use of *instance* means *presence* although he seems to be describing Cassius' manner or demeanor.

5. Brutus comments upon the characteristic temperament of hollow men who put up a great show but don't carry it out.

6. Cassius is angry because his judgment was treated as unimportant.

7. Brutus' point to Cassius here is that when Cassius condones corruption, punishment seems absent.

8. In the middle of their argument, Brutus tells Cassius he'll have to listen to even more assaults on Cassius' character even though it may annoy him to death.

9. Brutus points out that Cassius is irritably impatient.

10. Cassius uses the word as a synonym for *annoy*. Cassius asks Brutus whether his only function is to provide Brutus with laughter when he's troubled.

Act V

1. The messenger suggests that Brutus and Cassius' army marches bravely to battle.

2. Ensign is the battle flag or banner that identifies the army. Because these banners were suspended from horizontal supports, the eagles could perch on them.

3. To spoil is to plunder. Brutus' army probably took anything of value from the bodies of the dead or dying soldiers they defeated.

4. Create or produce. Messala comments upon how erroneous information never leads to a happy outcome.

5. Misinterpreted.

VOCABULARY REVIEW QUIZZES

Act I		Act II		Act III	
1.	C	1.	B	1.	A
2.	B	2.	D	2.	C
3.	A	3.	B	3.	C
4.	C	4.	D	4.	A
5.	C	5.	A	5.	C
6.	A	6.	D	6.	B
7.	C	7.	C	7.	A
8.	B	8.	A	8.	B
9.	D	9.	D	9.	C
10.	A	10.	B	10.	A

Act IV		Act V	
1.	A	1.	A
2.	C	2.	A
3.	A	3.	B
4.	C	4.	D
5.	A	5.	A
6.	C		
7.	D		
8.	B		
9.	D		
10.	C		

Appendix D

BIBLIOGRAPHY

Abcarian, Richard and Marvin Klotz, eds. *Literature: The Human Experience.* rev., shorter ed. New York: St. Martin's, 1984.

Allen, Grant and George C. Williamson. *Cities of Northern Italy: Verona, Padua, Bologna, and Ravenna.* Vol. 2. Boston: L.C. Page, 1906.

Barnet, Sylvan, Morton Berman, and William Burto, eds. *An Introduction to Literature: Fiction, Poetry, Drama.* Glenview: Scott, Foresman, 1989.

Bleich, David. *Readings and Feelings: A Guide to Subjective Criticism.* Urbana: National Council of Teachers of English, 1975.

Brockett, Oscar G. *History of the Theater.* Boston: Allyn and Bacon, 1968.

Brown, Hazel and Brian Cambourne. *Read and Retell: A Strategy for the Whole-Language / Natural Learning Classroom.* Portsmouth: Heinemann, 1987.

Cambourne, Brian. *The Whole Story: Natural Learning and the Acquisition of Literacy in the Classroom.* New York: Ashton-Scholastic, 1989.

Christenbury, Leila A. and Patricia P. Kelly. *Questioning: The Path to Critical Thinking.* ERIC/RCS Theory and Research into Practice (TRIP) Monograph Series. Urbana: NCTE, 1983.

Fox, Levi. *William Shakespeare: A Concise Life.* Norwich, England: Jerrold Printing, 1991.

Hamilton, Edith. *Mythology: Timeless Tales of Gods and Heroes.* New York: Mentor Books, 1942.

Julius Caesar in *William Shakespeare: The Complete Works.* Ed. Charles Jasper Sisson. New York: Harper & Row, 1953: 940–968.

Lee, Charlotte and David Grote. *Theater: Preparation and Performance.* Glenview: Scott, Foresman, 1982.

Miller, Bruce E. *Teaching the Art of Literature.* Urbana: National Council of Teachers of English, 1980.

Mizner, Arthur, ed. *Teaching Shakespeare: A Guide to the Teaching of Macbeth, Julius Caesar, The Merchant of Venice, Hamlet, Romeo and Juliet, A Midsummer Night's Dream, Othello, As You Like It, Twelfth Night, Richard II, Henry IV: Part One, The Tempest.* New York: The New American Library, Inc., 1969.

Muir, Ramsey. *Muir's Atlas of Ancient & Classical History.* 2nd. ed. New York: Barnes and Noble Inc., 1956.

Robinson, Randal. *Unlocking Shakespeare's Language.* ERIC/RCS Theory and Research into Practice (TRIP) Monograph Series. Urbana: NCTE, 1989.

Stanford, Judith A. *Responding to Literature.* Mountain View: Mayfield Publishing, 1992.

Vaughn, Joseph L. and Thomas H. Estes. *Reading and Reasoning Beyond the Primary Grades.* Boston: Allyn and Bacon, 1986.

Willek, Rene and Austin Warren. *Theory of Literature.* 3rd ed. New York: Harcourt, Brace & World, Inc., 1970.

Appendix E

VERSIONS OF *JULIUS CAESAR* AVAILABLE ON VIDEOTAPE

Julius Caesar. (1953). Marlon Brando, John Gielgud, and James Mason. Black and White. 120 minutes.

Julius Caesar. (1970). John Gielgud, Richard Chamberlin, Jason Robards, and Charlton Heston. Color. 116 minutes.

Julius Caesar. (1979). BBC/PBS production for "Shakespeare's Plays" series. Richard Rasco, Keith Michell, and Charles Gray. Color. 161 minutes.

Availability and Cost

BBC/PBS versions are generally available through larger video rental chains, state or regional public library, or state or regional educational film/media service libraries. Check with your school's librarian or media specialist.

Cost to purchase these video versions range from $25–$100.

The Writing Company issues a special Shakespeare Catalog. The Writing Company, 10200 Jefferson Boulevard, Culver City, CA 90232.

All versions listed above are available at present from Filmic Archives, The Cinema Center, Botsford, CT 06404. 1–800–366–1920.